I Almost Left Islam

How I Reclaimed My Faith

~

Umm Zakiyyah

I Almost Left Islam: How I Reclaimed My Faith

By Umm Zakiyyah

Copyright © 2017 by Al-Walaa Publications.
All Rights Reserved.

ISBN: 978-1-942985-12-9
Library of Congress Control Number: 2017943949

Order information at ummzakiyyah.com/store

Verses from Qur'an adapted from Saheeh International, Darussalam, and Yusuf Ali translations.

Published by Al-Walaa Publications
Camp Springs, Maryland USA

Glossary of Arabic Terms

adab: Islamic etiquette or manners
alhamdulillah: "All praise belongs to God"
Allah: the Arabic word for "God"
awliyaa': believers whose *emaan* and *taqwaa* grant them the honor of Allah calling them His beloved "friends" (singular: *wali* or *walee*)
ayah: a part of Qur'an or sign from God
ayaat: plural of *ayah*
bid'ah: religious innovation
bi'idhnillaah: "with the help or permission of Allah"
da'wah: teaching about Islam; inviting others to Islam
deen: a person's way of life rooted in beliefs about the ultimate purpose of life and the concepts of right and wrong
dhikr: remembrance of Allah, a prescribed in the Qur'an and Sunnah
du'aa: prayerful supplication or informal prayer
emaan: faith or authentic spiritual belief
fatwa: religious "ruling" by a scholar
fitnah: severe trial or temptation
ghusl: ritual bath
haraam: prohibited or forbidden; any act that has the possibility of punishment in the Hereafter
hijrah: migration from one place to another for the sake of one's soul
ijmaa': complete scholarly consensus in Islam dating back to the Companions of the Prophet (peace be upon him)
ikhtilaaf: scholarly disagreement
insha'Allah: "God-willing" or "if God wills"
Istikhaarah: supplication and voluntary prayer made when making a decision regarding something
kaafir: disbeliever
kuffaar: plural of *kaafir*
kufr: disbelief
Laa ilaaha illa Allah: the Muslim testimony of faith; "nothing has the right to be worshipped except God alone"
madhhab: official school of thought
mahram: close family member or relative
naseehah: sincere religious advice
niqaab: face veil
qadr: divine decree or predestination
riyaa: insincerity; showing off; doing anything to seek the admiration or approval of creation instead of Allah
saheeh: authentic (the highest form of authenticity for a hadith)
Salaah: obligatory prayer performed five times each day: *Fajr, Dhuhr, Asr, Maghrib,* and *Ishaa*
sallallaahu'alayhi wa sallam: "May peace and blessings be upon him"
Shaytaan: Satan or the Devil

shirk: assigning divine attributes to creation or creation's attributes to Allah; giving to creation any rights that are solely for Allah; worshipping anything or anyone along with or instead of Allah; paganism or idol worship
sihr: often translated as "black magic"; humans voluntarily working with jinn to bring benefit or harm to their own lives or that of others
tafseer: explanation of the meanings of Qur'an
tajweed: rules of reciting the Qur'an
taqleed: blind following
taqwaa: sincerely guarding oneself from the punishment of Allah
tasweer: images
tawakkul: complete trust in Allah
Tawheed: Oneness of Allah; Islamic monotheism
'ulamaa: scholars or people of knowledge
ummah: Muslim community
waswas: whisperings of *Shaytaan* that incite toxic self-doubt
wudhoo': ablution
zakaah: obligatory charity paid on one's wealth
zeenah: beautification or adornment
zina: fornication or adultery

*For those still holding on, even if only barely,
but don't want to let go.*

"Islam is submission, yes. But it is more than that. It is a relentless fight till death—against oneself—to save one's soul."
— from the journal of Umm Zakiyyah

◆

"For some of us, the only way we'll get our spiritual priorities straight is having our entire world collapse…until the only thing that allows us to stand is the bare minimum we need to survive—the pillars of life and faith. Then and only then will we truly understand Laa ilaaha illa Allah, *and the necessity to leave everything else alone, except what contradicts this."*
—from the journal of Umm Zakiyyah

A Burdened Soul

♦

This isn't a story I am proud of, and it's not one I ever planned on writing. It's not even one I planned on living. When I was younger, I imagined that leaving Islam was a logical process, one arrived at through careful analysis of Islamic beliefs and finding in them something inherently contradictory or something that one disagreed with. Thus, I never really comprehended it, and it consistently confounded me. How could a person go from believing in only God and worshipping Him alone to disbelieving in Him and worshipping creation instead of Him? It just didn't make any sense.

I remember being deeply intrigued by the story of a famous NFL player who had left Islam and converted to Christianity. I was never a football fan, but as a youth, I had been a fan of his, mainly because he was both a star player and a practicing Muslim. When I'd heard that he had converted to Christianity, I dismissed it as an absurd rumor, it was so unbelievable. The media was in the habit of taking sensational stories and making them front-page "news" with little to no regard for authenticity or credibility. I'd assumed this was what had happened with the football player. Or at least I was hoping so—because the alternative was too difficult to fathom.

In my young mind, it was impossible to go from being a "devout Muslim" to worshipping one of Allah's prophets and declaring this *shirk* as the only way to Heaven. Some months before, I had read a magazine feature about the NFL player in which he explained Islam to the readers and discussed the significance of the five daily prayers. I remember the piece really touching my heart. So it was difficult to reconcile this inspirational image with someone leaving Islam.

Months later, I was watching television and happened upon a Christian talk show in which the host said that today's guest would be the NFL player telling the story of why he'd left Islam. Naturally, this caught my attention, and I waited to see if the athlete would really be there. Eventually, he came on to the set, and the first thing I noticed about him was how visibly uncomfortable and fidgety he was. I watched as he kept glancing over his shoulder as if he expected someone to walk in and "catch him" there, though I'm sure he was fully aware that he was on national television.

When the host asked what inspired his decision to leave Islam for Christianity, the NFL player said, "When I was Muslim, I always felt guilty when I sinned. Now that I'm Christian, I don't feel guilty anymore because I know Jesus died for my sins."

I was only a teenager at the time, but I felt like it was the stupidest thing I'd ever heard. I nearly laughed out loud for how ridiculous this man's reasoning was. *So you want to get drunk and sleep with multiple women without the guilty conscience?* I shook my head in humored disbelief.

But at least his decision made sense to me now. I had been waiting for some profound reflection on how he'd happened upon some groundbreaking "evidence" that God was now a man in flesh and part of a Trinity instead of the Creator who was completely separate from His creation and who shared no kinship to them. I couldn't imagine what that "evidence" would entail, but at the time, it was the only logical reason my mind could accept for leaving the worship of God alone.

However, after hearing the NFL player's explanation, I understood his soul's desperate longing to live life without the burden of regret, self-correction, or personal accountability for his wrongs. Nevertheless, though I myself still had a lot to learn about life, I knew that even many devout Christians would find the man's reasoning problematic. Till today, I find the reasoning problematic myself.

But the man's story no longer confounds me.

It terrifies me.

Because I know how close I myself came to allowing my own soul to become "unburdened" by giving up on myself and my Lord.

I still haven't found all the words to explain exactly what was happening to me during this time. But in this book, along with the video series *I Almost Gave Up*, I pinpoint ten spiritual struggles that I faced during that time, along with ten solutions that I implemented to weather the most tumultuous spiritual storm of my life.

1
Do I Have the Right To Exist?

"The cycle of dysfunction and abuse begins to break when you no longer seek their love, permission, or approval. Or their forgiveness for the crime of existing—and choosing life and happiness for yourself."
—from the journal of Umm Zakiyyah

Behavior control, mind control, and soul control. This is what I was taught about my ultimate purpose in life. I was taught that there were certain people who had a greater right to my life choices, private thoughts, and deep spirituality than I did. I was even taught that they came before God Himself, or that they represented God Himself.

Wherever I went—whether I was at home learning about the rights of parents and family, at the masjid learning about the divine gifts of our community imam and my responsibility to dedicate my life to him, at school learning about the superiority of democracy over all political systems and my obligation to live and die for a flag, at gatherings of African-Americans talking about what I owed "our people" due to all they had suffered, or on the receiving end of the constant verbal abuse and harassment by atheists and "secularists" who blamed me and my religion for all the evil in the world—I heard the same message over and over again: *You don't have the right to exist. You have no right to your life, mind, or soul. I know what's best for you, and should you doubt that I'm right, God (or the Universe) will punish you—and you'd deserve it.* No one used these exact words, but the message was clear nonetheless. If I were to summarize in three words how my mind and heart processed all of these messages, it would be this: *You don't matter.* And I'd believed it.

Ironically, I'd always imagined that my thoughts and beliefs were rooted in praiseworthy self-sacrifice "for the sake of Allah," not in disappearing myself from existence. I loved my parents and family, I loved my religion and imam, I loved my heritage and people, and I loved my culture and country. So why shouldn't I continuously sacrifice for them?

Unless I genuinely believed that doing so would displease God or harm my life and soul—or that of others.

It would take years of emotional suffering and mental torment, of self-doubt and toxic shame, and nearly leaving Islam before I came to realize the power—

and threat—in this seemingly obvious exception. For it is in honoring this simple exception (to put one's soul and emotional health before anything else) that creates the dividing line between respect and abuse, freedom and tyranny, and human rights and oppression.

Herein lies the power of this exception, and its threat. Those who genuinely wish good for you in this world and understand (and respect) the rights of the human soul and its Creator will honor this exception willingly and humbly, as they know that, should they violate this divine exception, they are not only harming their own souls but also disrupting divine justice on earth.

It is not without immeasurable divine wisdom that God Himself has expressly forbade compelling another human soul to believe in something or live a life path that he or she genuinely believes is wrong or harmful (to the self or others), even if the person himself is sincerely mistaken. Hence the oft-repeated but so often misunderstood *ayah* of Qur'an: **"There shall be no compulsion in deen."** (*Al-Baqarah*, 2:256).

Why I Almost Gave Up

As I mentioned in the introduction, this is not a story that is easy to put into words. However, when I look back at the first problem I faced during my spiritual crisis, I can safely say it was rooted in three things pulling me down:
1. I felt overwhelmed spiritually such that I feared I could no longer continue.
2. I felt that I didn't have the right to exist.
3. I found many Muslim communities to be sources of pain and institutionalized pride.

I Felt Overwhelmed Spiritually

During my spiritual crisis, Islam began to feel like an increasing list of doubtful, *haraam*, and religious obligations; and I couldn't keep up. I wanted to hold on to my *emaan*, and I knew that I needed to. But I felt like I couldn't.

Part of the problem was my desire to stay away from anything that could even possibly be wrong. As a result of this determination, I followed the strictest opinion on nearly every *ikhtilaaf* issue amongst the scholars. The following excerpt from my blog "Walking Guilty, the Weight of Doubt and Sin" paints a pretty accurate picture of what led to this spiritual exhaustion:

> I thought I had it all figured out. I know that sounds cliché, naïve even, but it's true. I wasn't going to compromise my soul. I wasn't going to open myself up to sin. I wasn't going to Hell with my eyes open. Yes, I knew it wouldn't be easy. I knew I'd have to sacrifice and struggle. And I knew there would always be that internal battle for sincerity that nobody could conquer perfectly in this life.

But I could at least protect my actions in some way.

The Prophet (peace be upon him) said, "The *halaal* (permissible) is clear and the *haraam* (forbidden) is clear, and between them are matters that are *mushtabihaat* [unclear or doubtful]. Whoever is wary of these doubtful matters has absolved his religion and honor. And whoever indulges in them has indulged in the *haraam*. It is like a shepherd who herds his sheep too close to preserved sanctuary, and they will eventually graze in it. Every king has a sanctuary, and the sanctuary of Allah is what He has made *haraam*. There lies within the body a piece of flesh. If it is sound, the whole body is sound; and if it is corrupted, the whole body is corrupted. Verily, it is the heart" (Bukhari and Muslim).

In my youthful zeal, I thought that staying away from doubtful and forbidden matters was as simple as doing what was "safest": following the strictest opinion so as to remove any possibility of falling into error or sin.

So that's what I did.

In my commitment to religious "safety," I broke all my music CDs and stopped listening to music, thinking, "It might be a sin." I questioned singing and dancing [even in my own home] because that too had been labeled as *haraam* by some scholars. I even tried to stop listening to nasheeds (songs without musical instruments) because "that was safest."

I donned the *niqaab* (the face veil), thinking, "It's certainly not wrong to wear it." I wore an over-the-head abaya and gloves, and even experimented with covering my eyes. And I even left America to "make *hijrah*", thinking, "I fear for my soul in a non-Muslim society."

And though I loved to read, I even stopped reading novels for fear of "wasting time." I stopped giving speeches in front of men because, allegedly, that was a *fitnah* (severe temptation) for men. I stayed away from co-ed gatherings because I didn't want to "intermingle." I stopped taking and keeping pictures, and contemplated throwing away my family photos because "pictures are *haraam*." I questioned my calligraphy wall art because it "might be disrespecting the Qur'an." I stopped reading the Qur'an during my menses because menstruating women were "unclean."

And, believe it or not, the list goes on…

I Felt I Didn't Have The Right To Exist

As I mentioned earlier, I felt the continuous obligation to erase myself as an individual believer with rights to my own mind, life and soul. The rights of my parents and family came before me, the rights of my imam and African-American community came before me, and even the rights of a random scholar I'd never met came before me because he was an "inheritor of the Prophet" who, via a *fatwa*, could dictate what I could or could not do even in the privacy of my own home and in my worship in front of Allah.

Interestingly, it was via these numerous fatwas that I learned the widespread anti-Black, anti-women, and pro-Arab supremacy ideologies that were being taught as Islam in many Muslim communities. I also learned of both the subtle and blatant scholar worship happening in the *ummah*. Some Muslims went as far as to teach that even the dreams of certain sheikhs had religious significance for the lives of "commoners" or laypeople. Though Allah protected me from falling into this particular misguidance due to my detailed study of true dreams in light of the Qur'an and Sunnah, my "for the sake of Allah" mindset had me believing that my mental and emotional health could be sacrificed in the service of religious scholars, as well as family, elders, and "my people." In this, I genuinely imagined that Allah would continuously reward me for this sacrifice, even if I were to (literally) drop dead in exhaustion as a result.

However, what made this period so disastrous spiritually was not only my continuous self-sacrifice, but also my being consistently punished for making the slightest effort at self-care or protecting my soul. Unfortunately, whenever I sought to put my soul and my Lord first, I was mistreated, slandered, or ostracized if my choice inconvenienced or offended anyone, especially if the person was an elder or religious leader. In other words, I continuously encountered Muslims, many who were in leadership positions, who viewed it as an affront and a sin to honor the divine exception that represents the dividing line between respect and abuse, freedom and tyranny, and human rights and oppression: **Whenever you genuinely believe that serving, pleasing, or obeying someone will displease God or harm your life and soul, honor your life and soul.**

Nevertheless, after being consistently punished for engaging in self-care, I began to doubt that I even had divine permission to engage in soul-preservation if it offended someone who was deemed more knowledgeable or more important than I was. For many years, whenever I sought to honor my God-given right to my own mind, life, and soul, a host of offensive labels were applied to me: disrespectful, ignorant, misguided, arrogant, feminist, Wahhabi, and even *Shaytaan* himself. The epithet often varied, but the message never did: *You don't have the right to exist outside the life that we [your superiors] have carved out for you.*

Whenever I explained that I was only trying to do what I genuinely believed God required of me or what was healthiest for my emotional and spiritual health, I received some variation of this indignant response, "Who do you think you are?"

In other words, I was consistently reminded that I didn't have the right to exist.

True Believers and Real Scholars

In the interest of fairness and honesty (especially given the nature of this book), before I go on, I think it is important to mention that during my more than fifteen years of studying Qur'an and Islamic studies, of traveling throughout America and living in Egypt and Saudi Arabia, and of being a part of dozens of different Muslim communities, Allah has indeed blessed me to meet some remarkable believers, from both laypeople and scholars. And these believers still hold a special place in my heart till today. Amongst them are both men and women, and believers of all colors and ethnicities.

In fact, due to all the emotional manipulation, harassment, and spiritual abuse I've experienced at the hands of so many other "practicing Muslims" and professed imams and scholars, I've grown to appreciate these true Muslims, imams, and scholars more today than I did when Allah first decreed that we crossed paths. It is by Allah's mercy that it is largely due to my experience with these kindhearted believers and my studies under these truthful and knowledgeable imams and scholars that I can so often quickly and seamlessly distinguish spiritual truth from religious falsehood, and genuine Muslim brotherhood and sisterhood from manipulative behavior control and self-serving abuse.

As I alluded to earlier and as I believe cannot be overemphasized, the difference between these groups and those who contributed to my ultimate emotional and spiritual trauma lay in their willingness to honor my divine right to not serve, obey, and please them *whenever I genuinely believed that doing so would displease Allah or harm my life and soul (or that of others).* Moreover, they themselves feared that interfering with this right would expose them to the punishment of Allah, as they readily and consistently admitted their own human fallibility and their inherent inability to always know what was right for me (or others), even as many were amongst the most celebrated and knowledgeable imams and scholars.

Nevertheless, as I've said on many an occasion: It takes only one shot to kill a person. In other words, we can live our entire lives surrounded by good, trustworthy people, and amongst them is only one corrupt person. Yet this one corrupt person could be the one who harms or wounds us irrevocably—or takes our life.

For me, this irrevocable harm occurred in Muslim communities that were consistently sources of pain and institutionalized pride. Unfortunately, these negative experiences were (and continue to be) more common than my interactions with ostensibly true believers and real scholars.

Muslim Communities As Sources of Pain

Throughout my life I experienced continuous emotional pain in many Muslim communities because I was taught that I didn't have the right to exist. In Muslim communities comprised of primarily immigrant Muslims to America and their descendants or of non-Americans when I was traveling throughout the "Muslim world," almost anything that was rooted in my American culture or African-American heritage (even if something as simple as a natural hairstyle or rhythmic poetry) was labeled as *haraam* or "imitation of the *kuffaar*." In the small African-American Muslim community I was part of during my youth, the Muslims responded to this widespread anti-Black racism by teaching us that we should learn only from African-American Muslims with no connection to immigrants' "cultural Islam."

I was further taught that I had blindly follow and obey our community's African-American imam and view him as having been directly taught by God with no human teachers or intervention. When I implemented the divine command to protect my life and soul from harm (due to some of the imam's teachings not being aligned with what I understood Allah required of me), I was swiftly punished, slandered, ostracized, and labeled a traitor.

As a woman in non-Afrocentric communities, I was taught that Allah's commandments of hijab had nothing to do with my own soul and spiritual health except insomuch as I ensured that no man ever sexually desired me—even if I was committing no sin. In other words, if my hijab was deemed "pretty" or if I myself was deemed "attractive" (even if I covered my face and wore no makeup or visible jewelry), I was in sin if I didn't alter my clothes (or presence) until random men no longer found me attractive or a source of *fitnah*.

Recently, I wrote about this experience in hopes of shifting the focus of hijab back to women's obligation to obey Allah for the sake of their souls irrespective of men's sexual attractions, and I was accused of introducing "the alien religion of feminism." However, this negative experience was just one in a long line of continuous slander and harassment by both men and women who believed that the definition of women's Islamic modesty rested more in the minds and desires of random men than in the Book of Allah and the prophetic teachings.

Institutionalized Pride in Our Communities

Personally, I generally feel anxious and distressed whenever someone calls me a scholar or a "student of knowledge." Other than the obvious fact that I deserve neither title, I fear for my soul should I ever think of myself as such. Though both titles are certainly honorable in their own right—specifically when they match the title Allah has written for us—I have too often seen "knowledgeable Muslims" utilize their religious titles as licenses to silence, harm, and control believers whom they deem as "laity" or "commoners."

In fact, it is my experience that self-professed scholars, imams, and sheikhs are at the forefront in teaching that non-scholars do not have the right to their own minds, lives, and souls—even when the non-scholar genuinely believes that doing what is being asked or commanded of them by these scholars would displease Allah or harm their life and soul in some way.

Naturally, there are many scholars and students of knowledge who are not guilty of this and who do indeed fit the description that Allah gives true scholars: "those who fear Allah." However, we would be remiss to ignore or deny the widespread havoc that corrupt, ignorant, and misguided scholars are wreaking on the *ummah*, even when they (sometimes) intend good.

Many scholars consistently teach more about common people's obligation to them as "people of knowledge" than about every person's individual obligation to Allah and their own souls. Many assign themselves and their friends and teachers as saints and *"awliyaa'* of Allah." They teach Muslims about the necessity of *taqleed* (blind following) more than the obligation of caution when obeying any human being other the Prophet (peace be upon him). They transmit as "prophetic revelation" and Islamic mandates information given to them in their dreams and that of their teachers and favored scholars in history. They openly criticize and slander those who do not wish to join their groups, those who make exceptions to obeying them and their "saints," and those who openly profess to believing their obligation is to Allah over any scholar, sheikh, or spiritual teacher.

Sihr, sexual abuse, *zina* (fornication and adultery), and a host of other sins are indulged in under the guise of "Islamic permission" being granted to these "saints", sheikhs, and scholars. Some teach that having in one's heart the desire to enter Paradise is a form of materialistic greed and misguidance that distracts believers from "the path of Allah." Others teach that acts of *shirk* and *bid'ah* (like grave worship and making pilgrimage to shrines) are permissible, and that people who disbelieve in Islam can enter Paradise. Some teach that commandments like hijab are no longer applicable in modern times, that twirling and dancing in a trance are valid acts of worship, that Allah's permission for plural marriage is no longer valid, that the stories of prophets in the Qur'an are allegorical and thus not real, and the list goes on.

As a result, many laypeople who fear for their souls are running from these groups and "sheikhs" in hopes of finding some spiritual authenticity on their own. However, as I myself experienced firsthand, many imams and scholars are responding to believers' natural self-care and soul-preservation by verbally abusing and slandering those who will not blindly follow them or join their groups and cults.

Meanwhile, discussions about the divisions between scholars and common people are consistently centered around laypeople's "disrespect" or "disregard" for people of knowledge; laypeople's devaluing of "established knowledge," and the evils of those who are not "formally trained" having the audacity to teach others about Islam—or even practice Islam on their own independent of a "spiritual teacher." In these circles, it is as if the word "scholar" is synonymous with "infallible" or "divine", and "layperson" with "obligation to blindly obey."

For these reasons (and others that warrant a separate book itself), I feel anxious and distressed whenever I hear Muslims speak about the obligations that laypeople have to scholars while failing to acknowledge the need of every believer to protect his or her own soul from ignorant, misguided, or corrupt scholars—and to take personal responsibility for their own lives and souls.

During my spiritual crisis, there were moments that I doubted my own sanity due to the widespread teaching that my mind, life, and soul did not belong to me and my Lord alone, but to random imams, scholars, and sheikhs who (allegedly) had more rights to them than I did.

In other words, the Muslim communities' constant practice of institutionalized pride—which equates "formal training" (or formal studying of Islamic sciences in a university) with authentic Islamic scholarship and with one's divine rights to dictate and control the lives of Muslims—made me doubt my ability to hold on to my Islam.

How I Reclaimed My Faith

"We are in a sad state as believers when anything that does not appear to be overtly praising scholars is viewed as disrespecting them. In this mindset, it is not scholars we are disrespecting, but ourselves. For the righteous scholars humbly embrace that they are fallible human beings, and thus do not desire—let alone expect—overpraise."
—from the journal of Umm Zakiyyah

◆

By the mercy of Allah, I always knew that obeying, serving, and pleasing any human being came secondary to obeying, serving, and pleasing my Lord. However, the mere widespread occurrence of overpraising scholars (which sometimes resulted in committing *shirk*)—especially amongst ostensibly intelligent and sincere Muslims—had the psychological effect of making me think, even if momentarily, that I was the one who was wrong. After all, what was the likelihood that *all* of these Muslims (some of whom were celebrated imams and scholars) could be wrong?

Of course, logically speaking, there were many other Muslims, including imams and scholars, whom I knew personally and were not involved in this misguidance and religious extremism. But in moments of doubt, I sometimes forgot they existed. Or worse, I'd wonder, *What if they're wrong too?*

However, even amongst those scholars who were not involved in overpraising themselves, there was the culture of "follow the strictest opinion for the safety of your soul," which also contributed to my spiritual crisis.

So what could I do to save myself?

Fortunately, the solution came to me as a simple epiphany when I was reminded of the words of Allah:

> **"And I only created jinns and humans that they may worship Me alone."**
> —*Adh-Dhaariyaat* (51:56)

In other words, this *ayah* was a reminder from Allah that I am not here on earth to serve and please creation, no matter how knowledgeable they are. I am here to serve and please the One who created me. And He is Allah, not scholars, imams, or sheikhs.

Remembering this reminded me of my true purpose in life and helped me refocus my attention where it truly belonged: toward worshipping and obeying Allah alone.

But What About the Rights of Scholars?

On the topic of understanding the proper place of scholars in Islam, I'll share some reflections from my journal that helped me stay away from falling into extremes, whether in overpraising (or blindly following) scholars, or that of disregarding their knowledge completely and my need of them:

> *"Indeed, the scholars are the inheritors of the prophets, for the prophets do not leave behind a dinar or a dirham for inheritance, but rather, they leave behind knowledge..." (Abu Dawud, Al-Tirmidhi). This is a well-known hadith, and from it we learn that the responsibility of the scholar is great, as he or she is entrusted with inheriting and subsequently passing on the wealth of knowledge left behind by the Prophet, peace be upon him. Thus, when we "follow" trustworthy scholars, we are only being directed to follow the Prophet himself. For the job of the scholar is only to share authentic knowledge gained from detailed study of the original teachings. And just as a trustee of an estate does not add or take away from the wealth with which he is entrusted, so does a trustworthy scholar leave the prophetic inheritance undisturbed—except to share the knowledge in full, as his or her role demands.*

> *Religious knowledge is rooted more in the heart than in the mind. As such, when Allah speaks about the 'ulamaa (people of knowledge), He speaks about their fear of Him, not their accolades and certificates from*

books, classes, and teachers: *"It is only those who fear Allah, amongst His slaves, who are* 'ulamaa*" (Qur'an, 35:28).*

Thus, our classes and teachers—and accolades and certifications—benefit us only insomuch as our hearts benefit us.

Reflect, O child of Adam, reflect!

Then repent and self-correct.

Students of misguidance are taught to not question human beings. Students of spiritual truth are taught to not question Allah.

Allah would never make the path to Paradise something that is equally the path to Hellfire. So to believe you are obligated to follow without question any religious personality other than Prophet Muhammad, sallallaahu'alayhi wa sallam, *not only violates divine principles; it also violates common sense. For how many religious personalities, past and present, call their followers to misguidance and disbelief? How then is it possible that our Lord would* obligate *us to follow someone without question—then place us in Hellfire if we die upon misguidance or disbelief?*

Your blind following of anyone *is the result of conscious, deliberate choice—while knowing full well you had other options, for better or worse.*

Own it.

Because on the Day of Judgment, you'll have no other choice.

Beware of Accepting Any Invitation To the Hellfire

As I discuss my realization of the need to take personal responsibility for my soul and to stay focused on my purpose in life, it is crucial that I mention the need for all of us to remain mindful of the consistent tests in life, specifically those that could affect our ultimate fate in the grave and on the Day of Judgment.

Undoubtedly, of the most serious trials we will face come as a result of our having—or neglecting to have—the knowledge, sincerity, and fortitude to turn down any and every invitation to the Hellfire, even when it comes from people we love and respect. I reflect on this in my journal:

During your lifetime, you'll be invited to the Hellfire many times. For the sake of your soul, refuse every time. In guarding your heart from accepting the invitation, be sure to focus more on principles than people—and don't be naïve enough to believe that this destructive invitation will always come in the form of obvious evil.

So how do we protect ourselves? Here are five points to remember:

1. **Authentic Islam is based on the teachings of the Qur'an and Prophet Muhammad (peace be upon him)**, as understood by the Companions and earliest Muslims, as there is no new Islam. Bear in mind that believing that it is allowed to introduce new interpretations of foundational principles, obligations, and clear matters of *halaal* and *haraam* is what laid the path for the People of the Book making entirely new religions with no connection to the teachings of the Prophets Moses and Jesus (peace be upon them).
2. **No human being other than the Prophet (peace be upon him) has authority to teach commandments or prohibitions in the religion** or introduce concepts that promise specific reward or punishment in this world or the Hereafter—no matter how knowledgeable, righteous, or saintly we imagine them to be.
3. **The role of the Islamic scholar is to teach what was revealed to Prophet Muhammad (peace be upon him)** of the Book (Qur'an) and the Wisdom (the Sunnah), nothing more, nothing less.
4. **No Islamic teacher or believer (other than the Prophet himself) has perfect knowledge of Islam**, even if his or her foundational understanding of the religion is correct. Thus, when we are studying our faith, we must constantly supplicate to Allah to allow us to benefit from what is truthful and to protect us from what is mistaken, no matter who our teacher is and no matter how much we love, trust, and respect him or her.
5. **Know that Allah has made the truth of His faith so clear** that every human being who hears the message of Islam, whether illiterate or scholarly, has the capacity to recognize it as true. Likewise, every human being who accepts Allah's religion has the ability—and the obligation—to recognize and reject religious falsehood being taught as Islam, no matter whom or where it comes from. In this vein, know that we will all be held accountable on the Day of Judgment for our beliefs and actions, and we will not be able to blame our spiritual teachers or scholars for our own misguidance.

When in doubt, pray for guidance. Allah hears and answers all prayers.

And remember this: Many who rejected the Messengers in history were resentful that the Prophet whom Allah sent to them did not have the qualities they felt made him honorable and worthy of such a noble role, whether it was wealth, power, or a certain lineage. And many who followed misguidance in history were pleased with the "noble" traits of the one leading them to Hellfire, whether it was because the inviter was a parent, a "righteous" person, or someone they deemed honorable in some worldly way.

Today, we find history repeating itself in Muslims rejecting obvious spiritual truths because the person speaking the truth does not have a lofty scholarly title, did not study overseas or in an Islamic university, or is not part of our favored group, sect, or culture.

Be careful.

Many times Allah tests us by placing the truth on the tongue of one who will reveal to us the very depths of our hearts—and our response to this divine truth will make plain to us whether it is Allah or our pride that is most beloved to us in this world.

O dear soul, be careful.

O Allah! Make us recognize truth as truth and make us follow it, and make us recognize falsehood as falsehood and protect us from it! And O Allah, purify our hearts from the destructive diseases of pride, hatred, and envy! And make Your pleasure with us our highest priority in this world!

2

Why Am I Muslim?

◆

Our Agreement.

The agreement was
I was to accept the blows
And accept them quietly.
I was to show hurt
To ensure my shame
And to deny hurt
To protect their name
If they lied
I was to believe them
If they slandered me
I was to repent
If there was pain
(And there always was)
I was to cry in silence
And smile in front of the world
If I needed help
Love
Compassion
Or relief
I was to confide in the ones who hurt me
Or risk
Suffering beyond belief.

I wrote this poem while in a state of melancholy as I reflected on what I'd experienced in my life thus far as a result of taking to heart what I'd been taught about not having the right to exist. In my sincere ignorance and spiritual zeal, I had allowed myself to be mistreated and abused by those who claimed to love and care for me, and who claimed to have so much religious knowledge that I was obligated to do everything they said.

As I withstood the slander, emotional manipulation, and spiritual abuse, I was continuously reminded—often by the abusers themselves—of the rights these people had over me, as commanded by Allah Himself. Yet ironically, the reason I was continuously slandered and abused was that I consistently made exceptions to fulfilling the demands and desires of these people **whenever I genuinely believed that doing so would displease Allah or harm my life and soul.**

On many occasions, I would try to explain myself to them and give detailed, heartfelt explanations (and apologies) so that they wouldn't be offended by my life choices. But it was to no avail. I would be consistently asked, "Who do you think you are?"

So Why Am I Muslim?

It makes no sense to question one's spiritual path based on mistreatment by those who claim the same path. However, due to the combination of my spiritual exhaustion and emotional trauma, I began to question why I was Muslim. I don't have a detailed analysis of why this question weighed so heavily on me for so long, but it did. As a grappled desperately for an answer, I felt the dark waters of disbelief pulling me in, and I had no idea if I could keep my head above the water.

How I Reclaimed My Faith

"The people will see a time of patience in which someone adhering to his religion will be as if he were grasping a hot coal."
—Prophet Muhammad, peace be upon him
(Sunan al-Tirmidhī 2260, *saheeh* by Al-Albaani)

By Allah's mercy, this burden of grappling desperately for my faith was removed from my heart as my Lord reminded me Who He is and what it meant to be Muslim. *I am Muslim because I believe in Allah, my Creator, and because I know I have to meet Him,* my heart said.

During spiritual crisis, some people begin to doubt foundational principles like whether or not God exists, whether or not there is a Hereafter, and whether or not religion is in fact a farce, a tool invented by tyrannical humans to merely control the meek on earth. I was fortunate enough to never be burdened with the former two distresses, as even in my weakest moments, I knew I had a Creator and that I would meet Him in the Hereafter—even though I had a difficult time fighting the belief that I would end up in Hellfire no matter what I did.

However, there were moments that I began to question whether or not "religion" as it was popularly taught was in fact a human invention. Though religion was certainly not the only tool of control being utilized as a weapon of harm on earth, after politics and nationalism, it was definitely one of the most popular.

During this period of confusion, I penned this reflection in my journal: *The more I live the more I see how some Muslims use Islam as a tool of control instead of a religion of guidance.*

For some Muslims, simply reminding themselves that Islam is not defined by the actions of Muslims is enough to quell this spiritual doubt. However, though reminding myself of this obvious fact certainly helped, it was not enough. As I continuously met Muslims who mistreated others, especially those in authority over others—whether parents, spouses, or religious leaders—while claiming God commanded blind allegiance to them, I found it more and more difficult to live in theory. I realized that for myself, logic alone was not going to get me through this trial.

Nevertheless, pinpointing the inherent contradictions in anti-religion thinking did help. During this time, Allah decreed that I met Muslim apostates, secular Muslims, and those who had given up on believing in God and religion altogether. Ironically, listening to their tirades helped me see how utterly ridiculous the anti-religion doctrine was.

Of all of the senseless arguments I came across during that time, the easiest to refute was that of the atheists. Logic alone blew their arguments out the water. Here are some journal entries (some of which are intentionally sarcastic) that I wrote about this experience of refuting atheism and anti-religion as reasonable life paths:

Atheist Logic 101: If you don't believe in God, there are only two possibilities in life: If you are right and die an atheist, this life was all for nothing and you get absolutely nothing but a bed of dirt at the end. If you are wrong and die an atheist, this life was wasted and you get eternal Hellfire at the end. But for those who believe in God as He taught, there are only two possibilities: If we are right and die as believers, we fulfilled our purpose on earth and thus get eternal Paradise at the end. If we are wrong (as atheists claim), then we get absolutely nothing but a bed of dirt at the end—the *same* that atheists get in their BEST CASE scenario!
...So based on human logic alone, which would you choose?
1. You get absolutely nothing, or you get eternal Hellfire (dying upon atheism)
2. You get absolutely nothing, or you get eternal Paradise (dying upon belief)
...I'm not a rocket scientist, but my human logic tells me, number 2 wins EVERY time!'

You chose to stand where you are. No one forced you.

You can talk about all the horrible things you witnessed or experienced from people of religion. But doing so requires choosing to ignore and discount all the beautiful things you witnessed or experienced from people of religion—and all the horrible things you do yourself (though of course, you conveniently don't include your *faults and sins as stemming from non-religion).*

So don't tell me why you believe secularism, atheism, or whatever other falsehood is superior to religion. Because from a worldly perspective, every lifestyle has more than one vantage point—including a multiplicity of both good and bad. And you merely chose the one that allows you to convince yourself that no credible good exists in anyone else's.

Thus, you are a narcissist more than anything. And you chose to be.

It's amazing to me how emboldened secularists and anti-religion people feel in tearing down God and religion in the name of bettering the world. They use the painful experiences of themselves and others to justify this position, yet they ignore the painful experiences of those who have been abused and oppressed by the very secular and anti-religious systems they say will better the world.

You don't believe in God because many people have done evil in His name? You won't accept Islam because many Muslims have done evil in its name? So help me understand how your belief system works: Truth is a contest of participation. Whatever concept has the most participation by "good people" is right and true. Whatever concept has the most participation by "bad people" is wrong and false. So, generations ago, when people of God behaved better, God existed. Now, when people of God behave poorly, God ceases to exist. And, generations ago, when Muslims did much good for the world, Islam was true. So now that Muslims aren't known for much good, Islam is suddenly false. (With the added caveat, of course, that your "truth contest" proves God never existed and Islam was never true, based on the current results of your "contest of participation.") ...Well, matters of truth and faith are not popularity contests. But you'll find that out soon enough—when you die and discover that, unfortunately, eternal suffering does not cease to exist just because it has the most participation by "bad people."

❖❖❖

When you want something badly enough, God puts in front of you what reflects the deepest desires of your heart. If you want guidance, He will place before you righteous people and numerous means to attain spiritual tranquility and height. When you want sin and corruption, He will place before you misguided people and numerous means to attain the ugliness your broken soul makes you yearn for. If it is religion you resent, you will see an increasing number of "religious" people indulging in everything you loathe. And this will serve as proof that your turning away from God and religion was the right choice. Yet all you're seeing before you is a mirror of your own heart.

Religion Is Not a Game

People shouldn't play with religion. It's not a game. Or perhaps I should say people shouldn't play with the human soul. Because the souls of Allah's servants are not our personal playgrounds.

I prefer the terminology *human soul* instead of *religion* in this context because the former lessens the possibility of some of the more narcissistic people claiming themselves to be guilt-free since they don't ascribe to any "religion." Like the professional football player thinking a simple change in religion could protect him from accountability for wronging his soul, the anti-religion crowd believes that a simple change in labeling their ideology can protect them from culpability for crimes committed in the name of "religion." It is indeed confounding that humans actually imagine that abusing and harming others in the name of atheism, tolerance, or spreading "democracy" is any less evil than committing these same crimes in the name of "religion."

That is why I prefer to discuss the human soul instead of "religion." The truth is, however, that all humans have a religion. After all, a religion is merely a set of beliefs about one's purpose in life, and it is the ideology that ultimately defines our concepts of right and wrong. The human's "religion" does not always have a readily identifiable name or label—even to the one who ascribes to it—but it remains a religion nonetheless. In other words, a "religion" is a person's set of ideas, beliefs, and corresponding behavior that determine the experience of his or her human soul.

Muslims often say, "Islam is a way of life." And it is. But everyone's religion is a way of life, whether the person is conscious of this reality or not. Or perhaps I should say everyone's *deen* is a way of life—because that is what makes it a *deen*.

In the Qur'an, Allah commands the Prophet, peace be upon him (and by extension the believers) to say to the disbelievers, "For you is your *deen*, and for me is my *deen*" (*Al-Kaafiroon*, 109:6). Sometimes this Arabic term is translated as "religion," other times it is translated as "way." Irrespective of how the term in translated, what is being conveyed here is that Allah has created every human being such that he or she naturally lives upon a *deen*, a way of life that directly affects the state of his or her human soul.

This is why I say that people shouldn't play with religion—with the human soul. Whenever we play with this spiritual world, we are wedging ourselves between a person and his or her Lord.

What Helped Me Most

In the end, what helped me most in getting through this difficult period was reading and reflecting on the Words of Allah. Just reading how He described Himself reminded me that He is not merely "out there" somewhere with no meaningful connection to His creation. And while His name is certainly used as an excuse by corrupt people to do evil, my heart knew that there were specific things He had asked of me while I was on earth, irrespective of how others responded to His commands.

I could label the spiritual path He obligated for us as "religion" or I could label it as something else. Either way, I would be held accountable for living according to it.

But Allah had called it "Islam." And that's why I was Muslim.

Allah says what has been translated to mean:

"He is Allah, other than whom none has the right to be worshipped, Knower of the unseen and the witnessed. He is the Entirely Merciful, the Especially Merciful. He is Allah, other than whom there is no deity, the Sovereign, the Pure, the Perfection, the Bestower of Faith, the Overseer, the Exalted in Might, the Compeller, the Superior. Exalted is Allah above whatever they associate with Him."
—*Al-Hashr* (59:22-24)

3
Stressed and Confused

♦

"Most of us who have felt we could no longer be Muslim don't share our pain or struggles with the world. Most just quietly retreat into the background of the mundane tasks of life, suffering in a quiet bitterness that wears at the spirit and soul."
—from the journal of Umm Zakiyyah

When I came close to giving up on practicing Islam, my heart and mind were cluttered with things that were consistently causing me stress and spiritual confusion. Though I had reminded myself of who my Lord was, what my ultimate purpose in life was, and why I was Muslim; I still could not pull myself out of my stress and confusion.

All around me people were discussing religion like it was a topic for a debate, instead of a life path designed to purify our souls in preparation to meet our Creator. Amongst Muslims, men and women argued about which group or sect one should join or stay away from, and I found myself feeling more and more distant from my brothers and sisters in Islam. As I listened to their arguments, I was consistently reminded of this hadith narrated by the Companion Hudhayfah ibn al-Yaman, may Allah be pleased with him:

> "People used to ask the Prophet (peace be upon him) about good things, but I used to ask him about bad things because I was afraid that they might overtake me. I said, 'O Messenger of Allah, we were lost in ignorance (*jahiliyyah*) and evil, then Allah brought this good (i.e. Islam). Will some evil come after this good thing?' He said, 'Yes.' I asked, 'And will some good come after that evil?' He said, 'Yes, but it will be tainted with some evil.' I asked, 'How will it be tainted?' He said, 'There will be some people who will lead others on a path different from mine. You will see good and bad in them.' I asked, 'Will some evil come after that good?' He said, 'Some people will be standing and calling at the gates of Hell; whoever responds to their call, they will throw him into the Fire.' I said, 'O Messenger of Allah, describe them for us.' He said, 'They will be from our own people, and will speak our language.' I asked, 'What do you advise me to do if I should live to see that?' He said, 'Stick to the

main body (*jamaa'ah*) of the Muslims and their leader (imam).' I asked, 'What if there is no main body and no leader?' He said, 'Isolate yourself from all of these sects, even if you have to eat the roots of trees until death overcomes you while you are in that state'" (Sahih Muslim).

Whenever I would think of this hadith, it calmed my heart, as it was a reminder that I was doing the right thing by striving my level best to stay away from sectarianism. I knew it was impossible to get everything right, but I also knew that Islam was more about striving than actualizing. As I reflected on this ongoing spiritual struggle in life, I penned this entry in my journal:

In the end, Islam is about striving, not actualizing. We strive to follow the Qur'an and Sunnah...though we'll never "actualize" this goal perfectly. We strive against falling into sin, but we'll never avoid sin completely. But this is not a problem. This is the point.

Islam is about earning Allah's Mercy and Forgiveness, not about overcoming our humanity.

Those who suffer most from spiritual turmoil, in my view, are those who view human imperfections as problems, and the definition of practicing Islam as achieving perfection.

Naturally, this non-sectarian life path required constant *du'aa* and asking Allah's guidance. I had already gotten in the habit of praying *Istikhaarah* before making any decision, even if only to attend a certain Islamic class, to go to a certain event, or even to follow a particular scholarly point of view on a topic. And this proved to be very helpful when I was stressed and doubting myself.

Whenever I was in the company of others, I strove to focus all discussions of religion on the goal of clarifying truth and staying away from falsehood, irrespective of which sect, group, or personality spoke the truth or had fallen into falsehood. Though on the surface, this sounds like a pretty safe course of action, many Muslims found this line of reasoning misguided, as they insisted I had to commit to a particular group or single school of thought in order to worship Allah properly. However, I would calmly explain that my goal was simply to be Muslim as defined by Allah in the Qur'an and prophetic Sunnah so that I could enter Paradise after I died, *bi'idhnillaah*.

"You're living in a fantasy!" one woman said to me before declaring that I *had* to formally attach myself to a specific religious group or sect. "You can't be 'just Muslim'!" I then asked her: "To you or Allah?" She had no response.

Conversations like these reminded me of why religious labels (other than *Muslim* and *believer*) scared me so much. This woman had associated Islam with manmade groups for so long that she'd forgotten that being Muslim was only about you and Allah. Yes, as I told her, I knew that *humans* would categorize me, thus placing all sorts of labels next to my name. But I was concerned with only what was written next to my name in front of Allah.

In reflecting on how scary it was to fall into misguidance with respect to finding safety in religious labels, I penned this note to myself in my journal:

Dear soul, know this, and know it well. You are never safe. It doesn't matter what group you've attached to, what spiritual teacher praises you, or what praiseworthy label you've put on yourself. You have no guarantee of protection from misguidance or even disbelief.

In fact, we are most susceptible to these spiritual tragedies when we think we are safe from them. Remember, it was arrogance and self-satisfaction that destroyed Iblis, not attaching himself to the wrong group, teacher, or label.

But no one and nothing—and I mean absolutely no one and nothing—can do your soul-work on your behalf.

Have faith, yes, but do not become comfortable. Until your soul is seized and you have received the glad tidings that your Lord is pleased with you, you are never safe.

Despite my ostensible fortitude in living according to only what Allah required of me, I felt alienated from most Muslims around me. Periodically, I would try to go to Islamic classes to lift my *emaan*, but most times I returned home feeling worse than when I'd left. Most classes spent more time talking about issues of *ikhtilaaf* (or about why their group or sheikh was better than another group or sheikh) than about foundational and clear matters that were necessary to reinvigorate and strengthen our *emaan*.

Prophet Muhammad (peace be upon him) said, "*Emaan* wears out in one's heart, just as the dress wears out (becomes thin). Therefore, ask Allah to renew *emaan* in your hearts" (*Mustadrak Al-Hakim*, authentic). I knew my *emaan* was wearing thin, so I was going to classes in hopes of having it renewed by the reminders of Allah. But unfortunately, I would attend classes and hear more praises of certain scholars and sheikhs than of Allah Himself. I'd also hear more quotes from these scholars and sheikhs than those from Prophet Muhammad (peace be upon him). Often Allah and His Prophet were mentioned only to justify what was being taught from or about a particular scholar or sheikh.

I cannot speak for anyone else going through spiritual crisis, but this "*dhikr* of human beings" did not help my *emaan*. Perhaps, for others hearing the lofty traits of certain scholars reminded them of the beauty of Islam. However, for me, it reminded me of how I was so often guilted into following the words of men over the Words of Allah. I simply could not understand what was so hard about sharing the teachings from the Qur'an and Sunnah regarding the Hereafter, the specific supplications we can make during difficult times, the blessings of the night prayer, and so on. These reminders were what my heart was yearning for.

But I'd often go home empty handed, and my *emaan* would drop even more. I eventually gave up on attending Islamic classes altogether except the ones I had with my Qur'an teachers, with whom I studied *tajweed* and *tafseer*.

However, it remained difficult withstanding the criticism of those who felt that my absence in certain classes or groups (or that my discomfort with hearing the praises of certain scholars more than the praises of Allah) was indicative of religious misguidance. Moreover, I still had to interact with the world around me, and anti-Muslim bigotry was increasing manifold, especially amongst atheists and anti-religion extremists who felt emboldened to harass and mock people of faith at every opportunity. In reflecting on this trial, I wrote this journal entry:

This is a lonely journey, I cannot lie. Holding on to your faith, I mean. It's not supposed to be. But it is. It sometimes feels as if making the decision to practice Islam openly is a contractual agreement between you and the rest of the world, saying that it's completely okay for them to make your life miserable—emotionally, psychologically and practically. That it's completely okay for them to follow and announce your faults. That it's completely okay for them to blame you for everything that's gone wrong in the name of God and religion. That it's completely okay for them to harass, abuse, and bully you—while you aren't allowed to have even unspoken *beliefs that they find offensive. And that it's completely okay for those closest to you—whether through the bond of faith, friendship, or blood—to watch you suffer and say you deserved it. Because you had the audacity to make others uncomfortable by holding on to your faith at all.*

But I don't intend to paint myself as a victim, because I am not. I mention these trials only to illustrate the spiritual difficulties I was going through at the time. In fact, some of my most difficult moments came when I reflected on my past behavior and wondered how many people I had inadvertently hurt during my own period of spiritual zeal. I too had been a student of books and classes who had been taught to disregard intuitive human empathy in favor of rehearsed *naseehah* borrowed from humans' "religious scripts." As I regretted my own unwitting participation in other people's pain, I penned the following entry in my journal, as I shared in my book entitled *Pain*:

Oh, the script, that religious script,
the one handed to every student of books and classes,
who reads his lines carefully,
then takes the stage,
declaring what is right or wrong in the life of the
unfortunate souls who find themselves the unwitting
audience of their own lives.

How I Reclaimed My Faith

"O Allah, I am Your servant, child of Your male servant, child of Your female servant; my forelock is in Your hand. Your command over me is forever executed and Your decree over me is just. I ask You by every name belonging to You which You name Yourself with, or revealed in Your Book, or You taught to any of Your creation, or You have preserved in the knowledge of the unseen with You, that You make the Qur'an the life of my heart and the light of my breast, and a departure for my sorrow and a release for my anxiety."
—Du'aa for anxiety and sorrow as taught by Prophet Muhammad, peace be upon him
(Al-Albaani, *as-Silsilah as-Saheehah*, 199)

As I prayed to Allah to remove the stress and confusion from me, I knew that I needed to clear the clutter from my mind and heart because it was distracting me from Allah. Although I had reminded myself that I needed to concern myself with only my Lord, having my *heart* aligned with this noble focus was a different task entirely. In achieving this, I understood that there was no option but to continuously ask Allah for help and find some semblance of peace in the struggle. In my journal I wrote:

There are no shortcuts to purifying the heart. There are no shortcuts to patience. And there are no shortcuts to Paradise. Do the work, and embrace the daily, harrowing struggle of living upon the Siraatul-Mustaqeem *(the Right Path).*

In reminding myself to stay focused on what was most important, I also wrote: *If you're struggling in your faith, this is my advice to you: Remove the excess baggage and carry only the burdens your Lord has given you.*

Though this reminder was extremely helpful, I found that one of the most difficult aspects of working through spiritual crisis was that you couldn't just skip over the stress and confusion, even when you knew where you needed to be. The pain and agony are parts of the healing journey itself, so there was no choice but to bear them with patience. Upon realizing this difficult reality, I wrote this note to myself in my journal:

Let it hurt.
The only way out of spiritual crisis is through it.
So vent your frustrations, and cry your confusion to your Lord.

I also wrote: *It's not always about a problem to be solved. Sometimes it's about a struggle to be embraced.*

Part of the pain of the struggle is pushing yourself to do the things you know you need to do while knowing it would be burdensome. During this time, one of those most difficult tasks for me was reading the Qur'an. The truth is, I didn't want to read it, but I forced myself. I knew that I would only complicate my struggle if I couldn't bring myself to read at least one *ayah* of my Lord's Words each day. To some people, this may sound like so little, and maybe it is. But for me, achieving this was momentous.

I was also terrified that if I didn't read the Qur'an each day, Allah would remove from me the ability to read and understand what I was reading. Arabic was not my native language, and it had taken me many years to be able to open the Qur'an and read it without the assistance of transliteration or listening to a reciter. I was still learning a lot of the vocabulary, but I knew having the ability to read Qur'an in the language it was revealed and with correct *tajweed* was a tremendous gift that I did not want taken from me.

Who Is Your Lord?

During some of my more difficult moments of anxiety and stress, I had to keep reminding myself of why I was on earth. *Who is your Lord? What is your religion? Who is your prophet?* Sometimes I would recite these questions to myself so that I could remember that it wasn't the people's opinions that I needed to worry about, but the answers to these questions.

Make your focus the commandments of Allah's Book first and foremost, I told myself, because in them, there is no doubt. This is where success lies.

At the beginning of the Qur'an, Allah says what has been translated to mean:

"Alif, Lam, Meem. This is the Book about which there is no doubt, a guidance for those conscious of Allah, who believe in the unseen, establish prayer, and spend out of what We have provided for them, And who believe in what has been revealed to you, [O Muhammad], and what was revealed before you, and of the Hereafter they are certain [in faith]. Those are upon [right] guidance from their Lord, and it is those who are the successful."
—*Al-Baqarah* (2:1-5)

As I stressed over all of the things people were saying I needed to focus on based upon the opinions of their group and spiritual teachers, I reflected on what I had studied in the *tafseer* of these *ayaat*, specifically where Allah says "...who believe in what has been revealed to you, [O Muhammad], and what was revealed before you."

The scholars of *tafseer* explained that the wording here indicated that there was no new revelation or religious teachings that we should focus on after what was revealed to Prophet Muhammad, peace be upon him. So no matter how knowledgeable someone was, I was obligated to them only insomuch as what they were teaching could be verified as coming from the teachings of the Prophet himself.

4

Stay Away From Doubtful?

♦

"Yes, this world is a prison for the believer. But that doesn't mean we have to build one for ourselves while we're here."
—from the journal of Umm Zakiyyah

Before my spiritual crisis, spiritual safety had always been an objective matter. It was something arrived at by looking at scholarly evidences derived from the Qur'an and Sunnah, and simply doing what could not *possibly* be wrong. And it had worked. I felt completely "safe" in nearly everything I did.

But there was only one problem (well, two actually): I was overwhelmed. And, truth be told, my *emaan*—the very faith I was trying to preserve through my "safety"—began to suffer.

Some might say that my staying away from what could even possibly be wrong was in fact preserving my soul. And that's possible. After all, the soul is essentially a matter of the Unseen, and we have no way of knowing if our soul has been preserved spiritually until we meet Allah. However, Allah does not leave us without signs, and I had at least two signs that my approach to "religious safety" was not healthy for my soul:

1. The more I sought to be "safe" (by overburdening myself), the more distant I felt from Allah and the more overwhelming and frustrating "practicing Islam" became to me.
2. The only way for me to avoid the exhaustion and frustration I was falling into was to make a conscious effort to remain ignorant of my religion. Why? Because I was only learning about these "doubtful" matters by voluntarily seeking knowledge through reading Islamic books, listening to Islamic lectures, and going to Islamic classes. Otherwise, I'd have no idea there existed a genuine difference of opinion on any of these issues.

What Went Wrong?

I think we all know the feeling. You go to an Islamic lecture inspired to be a better Muslim and then the speaker starts talking about things you never even considered to be wrong, let alone *haraam* or forbidden in Islam. And your heart drops and you think, "I'm a horrible Muslim." Because you're guilty of what they're talking about.

And after weeks of stressing and agonizing over your soul, you say to yourself, "Well, it's a doubtful matter, so it's best to stay away from it."

But it doesn't stop there. You give up one thing after the other, after the other, and after the other…

Until you feel like just giving up…

No, I'm not talking about religious safety that preserves your soul because you gave up something for the sake of Allah. I'm talking about "religious safety" that exhausts your soul because you were never convinced you had to give it up in the first place.

And chances are, though you're "safe" regarding this scholarly disagreement, your prayers are not consistent or performed with concentration; you don't spend much time in *du'aa*; you don't read the Qur'an every day; you don't fast much (if at all) outside of Ramadan; and you don't even give much charity.

But in seeking to be a "good Muslim," you somehow managed to make your biggest concern something else—by shifting the very definition of "religious safety" to the teachings of humans and away from the teachings of Allah and His Messenger.

Things They Said Are *Haraam* or Doubtful in Islam

I think we take a lot for granted when we caution people to stay away from what *we* view as *haraam* or doubtful in Islam when there are other permissible views on the issue. In such discussions, the concept of practicing Islam properly often becomes an intellectual exercise in logistics—or even an entertaining topic for debate—as opposed to an intimate, personally *lived* experience for the person we're talking to. As such, we assume what looks logically right or spiritually "safe" on paper is obviously right or spiritually safe in real life. And that's simply not the case.

And again, I'm not talking about foundational concepts, clear issues, or matters for which religious disagreement is not allowed. I'm talking about issues that, either due to their worldly nature or to scholarly debate in Islamic history, are not considered matters of *ijmaa'* (complete scholarly agreement since the time of the Companions and early Muslims) in Islam.

I don't have the words to explain how dangerous this simplistic view is, not only to the spiritual lives of believers, but also to the souls of those who use their tongues to spread their personal views as representative of what is always "right" or "safest" according to Allah Himself. And given that the terms "right" and "safest" have become synonymous with whatever is the absolute strictest view, this widespread simplistic view of Islam becomes even more of a concern.

"But the issues of *ijmaa'* are so few!" many Muslims have responded when I brought up the phenomenon of teaching non-*ijmaa'* issues as if they're inflexible

Islamic requirements instead of matters that have been subject to scholarly disagreement for centuries.

This response always puzzles me because I don't understand what the problem is here. It's as if we're saying, "No fair! If I'm stuck with telling Muslims they're wrong only when they definitely *are*, how will I fill the rest of my time when I'm telling them what to do?"

Don't get me wrong, I'm not saying it's wrong to advise Muslims about right and wrong on issues that are not foundational, clear or *ijmaa'*. What I'm saying is, when we *know* an issue is not as black-and-white as we're personally convinced it is (due to *our* research or conclusion on the topic), it is dishonest to present it as if no other point of view is allowed in Islam, thereby implying that a person is *definitely* falling into clear sin or *kufr* (disbelief) if they disagree with us.

What's so hard about saying, "I believe *xyz* because from my studies, it's most strongly supported by Islamic evidences. However, historically, the scholars of the Sunnah have disagreed on this"? In other words, what's so hard about being honest?

Guard Your Tongue

Today I shudder when I hear people teach Islam in this simplistic, inflexible way, implying or stating outright that the strictest point of view is always "safest" because it allegedly allows you to always stay away from sin or "doubtful matters" in Islam. Even if we forget for a moment that "doubtful matters" (*mushtabihaat*) do not represent a definitive category of topics or rulings in Islam—or that spiritual safety isn't found in external scholarly rulings so much as in the internal workings of the human soul—when we teach Islam in this manner, what does it do to a person's mind, spirit, and heart? And if the person believes us—as most who sincerely fear Allah would, because who wants to risk going to Hell?—what will their spiritual practice of Islam look like in the long run, if it exists at all?

This may sound like a question of existential philosophy, but I'm asking it sincerely in hopes that we will pause and reflect. Let us consider sincerely—bearing in mind that Allah is watching, the angels are writing, and we'll be held accountable for everything we teach in Allah's Name—what we're doing to each other while we use Allah's name to inflict spiritual wounds.

In Staying Away From Doubtful, I Almost Lost My Soul

I am not speaking in theory here. I was one of those sincere Muslim trying to stay away from everything that could even *possibly* be wrong or doubtful in Islam only to find myself scrambling to hold on to my *emaan*, my faith itself.

I've also been tested with being an advisor to Muslims facing spiritual crisis, to men and women on the verge of leaving Islam, to people who have already left Islam, to youth fed up with a religion that feels impossible to practice, and to Muslim women who genuinely believe that Islam is a religion that requires their suffering so that men will be happy.

And as I say often when I'm doing interviews or talks on this topic, "If you work in the withdrawal office at a school, what you see as important is going to be quite different from those who work in the office of admissions."

And I simply cannot find any Islamic evidences—or even convincing logic—that a person who *wants* to be a good, practicing Muslim cannot be simply because their Islamic practice does not adhere to the absolute strictest interpretation of a matter subject to permissible disagreement.

Religious Safety in Your Life

With a topic like this, I think it's helpful to give real life examples of what following the allegedly "safest" view looks like in real life for many people. For this reason, I've compiled a list (below) of matters that during my more than fifteen years of studying Islam in America and abroad, I've heard attributed to Islamic scholars or Islam itself as being *haraam*, or at the very least blameworthy or "doubtful" in Islam.

Sometimes I heard these things directly from Islamic teachers while sitting in their classes, sometimes in an Islamic book I was reading, sometimes from an Islamic Q&A website run by one or more Muslim teachers and scholars, sometimes from an Islamic teacher's video or audio lecture downloaded or accessed online, sometimes from a friend or family member who attended an Islamic class or lecture and shared what they learned, and sometimes from a fellow Muslim (most often one who viewed it as their religious obligation to "warn" or advise other Muslims, saying we're obligated to follow what their favored scholar or Islamic understanding had concluded on the matter).

As you read this list, bear in mind that I am not listing these things to suggest that *none* of these are matters better left alone for the safety of your soul. You know your life, circumstances, and weaknesses better than anyone else. As such, it is fully within your Islamic right—and is in fact your Islamic obligation—to stay away from *anything* that Allah has shown you is harmful to your soul.

Furthermore, as I strive to consistently advise: No matter what proofs exist for or against any point of view, we should *always* do what we sincerely believe Allah requires of us, no matter what anyone else says for or against it.

Sometimes this will be the strictest view, and sometimes the more lenient. But this does *not* mean that everyone's protection of their soul will look exactly like yours. Nor does it mean that what *you* view as doubtful or uncertain is automatically doubtful or unclear in the religion of Islam.

What the "Safest" (Strictest) View Looks Like in Real Life

In addition to the well-known permissible disagreement on the strict requirement for a woman to cover her face and the not so well-known permissible disagreement surrounding the strict prohibition against *all* music (even the daff outside of Eid and weddings), below is a list of things that I've personally encountered as being labeled as *haraam* (prohibited) or blameworthy in Islam.

If a person disagreed with the *haraam* label, they were often told, "It's better to stay away from doubtful matters," hence implying that even *if* the issue isn't *haraam*, they are displeasing Allah by delving into something that is considered "doubtful," thus disobeying the instructions of the Prophet, *sallallaahu'alayhi wa sallam*, to stay away from doubtful for the safety of our faith.

As you read the list, imagine two scenarios (and yes, these two scenarios do exist in real life):

1. A person is seeking to follow the strictest opinion on all Islamic disagreement because they sincerely believe this is what it means to be safe with regards to their religion in front of Allah.
2. A person who disagrees with any of these is told that they are following their desires and are evil, misguided, and spiritually corrupt for insisting on delving into matters that are "at best" left alone in Islam.

Here is an incomplete list of the allegedly *haraam* and blameworthy or "doubtful" matters that have been attributed to Islam and/or Muslim scholars of the past and present:

- Polygyny in modern times
- Polygyny in the West
- Divorcing a "good Muslim man"
- Divorcing a "good Muslim woman"
- Oral sex
- Having sex while naked (without clothes or without a blanket or sheet covering the husband and wife)
- Voice-only beats and compilations (if they sound like instruments)
- Listening to a cappella nasheeds (because today, Muslim artists allegedly harmonize their voices like Christians do in church)
- Any nasheeds (because the nasheeds of today aren't like the nasheeds of the past)
- Using a nice voice while singing a nasheed (because this is extravagance and imitation of the *kuffaar*)
- Supporting anyone who does nasheeds (because this is supporting the culture of the *kuffaar*)
- A woman listening to a man sing a nasheed (because it can make her think about him sexually)
- A man singing a nasheed (because he's like a homosexual)

- A man playing the *daff* (because it's imitating women)
- Singing songs at home to your children (because singing itself is "disliked" or *haraam*)
- All rap, even without music (imitation of the *kuffaar*)
- Hip hop, even without music (because it is evil and an imitation of the *kuffaar*)—but non-American Muslim cultural music is fine, even *with* instruments
- American songs, even without music or bad lyrics (imitation of the *kuffaar*)
- Afros (imitation of the *kuffaar*)
- Braids (imitation of the *kuffaar*)
- Locs (imitation of the *kuffaar*)
- Slang (imitation of the *kuffaar*)
- A woman not unbraiding her hair before performing *ghusl* (after menses or due to sexual relations with her husband)
- American clothes (imitation of the *kuffaar*)
- Buying American brands/products (supporting the killing of Muslims)
- Buying from any Jewish-owned business (because allegedly *all* Jews donate their money to support killing Palestinians)
- Reading any novels (wasting time)
- Writing novels (lying, wasting time, and misguiding people away from Allah)
- Having a photo of any living thing on the cover of a book, even if only partial or the face isn't showing
- Reading any book that isn't inherently religious (because it takes you away from the remembrance of Allah)
- Men playing sports (waste of time)
- Martial arts (because it allegedly requires *shirk* practices and beliefs)
- Yoga (because it allegedly requires *shirk* practices and beliefs)
- Women playing sports (makes men imagine them sexually)
- A woman running or exercising in public (because the quick movement makes her covered body parts move, or she becomes a *fitnah* for men)
- Women laughing in the presence of men (this is intermingling, flirting, or bad character)
- Girls playing with dolls (because the dolls are like idols or *tasweer*, forbidden images)
- Coloring books for children (because this is *tasweer*)
- Taking pictures (because this is creating *tasweer*)
- Living in the West
- Studying in the West
- Attending a co-ed school

- Speaking to a non-*mahram* person of the opposite sex about anything unless it's absolutely necessary (i.e. life and death)
- A woman initiating salaams to a man
- A woman speaking at all in the presence of a man
- A woman reciting Qur'an if there's even a *chance* a man can hear her
- A woman riding a bike (because the shape of her sitting body is immodest and a sexual *fitnah* for men)
- A woman driving a car (because this leads to *fitnah*)
- A woman appearing on TV, even if she's fully covered (leads to *fitnah* and allegedly forces men to look at her without lowering their gazes)
- A woman allowing her husband to go to sleep while he's upset with her, even if he wronged her
- Saying "I love you" to non-Muslim parents (because we're not allowed to love disbelievers)
- A woman wearing pants, even in the privacy of her own home (imitation of men)
- Jean fabric (imitation of the *kuffaar*)
- Suit and tie (imitation of the *kuffaar*)
- Having a Facebook account (leads to evil, social corruption and *haraam* interactions between men and women)
- Having Internet in your house (leads to evil, social corruption, and access to lots of *haraam*)
- Having and using the TV (because the images are *tasweer* and therefore *haraam*)
- A woman speaking in public, even in full hijab (makes men imagine her sexually)
- A woman having short hair (imitation of men)
- Men having long hair (imitation of women)
- A woman praying in public (because her *rukoo'* and *sujood* are immodest and these positions can be a *fitnah* for men)
- A woman wearing a coat over her abaya (it shows the shape of her body)
- A woman wearing colorful shoes (it's considered *zeenah* and attracts the attention of men)
- Gold buckles and zippers on a woman's purse or shoes (it's *zeenah* and attracts the attention of men)
- Women wearing gold jewelry, even if unseen (because there's a scholarly opinion that it's *haraam* for anyone to wear gold)
- Giving your children spankings (except when they refuse to pray)
- Women wearing rings or facial jewelry that can be seen in public (because this is a sexual *fitnah* for men)

- Women wearing bras (because it accents the shape of her breasts, even if she's covered)
- Women wearing kohl when her eyes are uncovered (because it's a sexual *fitnah* for men)
- A woman smiling near men (this is inappropriate and indicates lack of *adab*)
- Reading and reflecting on the Qur'an alone (because you're not a scholar and you don't have this right)
- Discussing the Qur'an with others (because you're not a scholar and you don't have this right)
- Teaching about Islam if you're not a scholar (because you could be misguiding people, even if you're not saying anything wrong)
- Brushing your teeth while fasting
- Hugging or kissing your husband or wife while fasting
- Using rubbing alcohol to sanitize your skin (because alcohol is *haraam*)
- Using your *'aql* (intellect or common sense) to help you determine what is right or wrong to do as a Muslim, even if your conclusion stays within the bounds of what's permissible in Islam
- Researching the scholarly evidences on a controversial issue to see which scholarly view you believe is right (because you are not a scholar so you're not allowed to research anything in Islam)
- Signing a book you wrote (because this is *riyaa*, imitation of the *kuffaar*, and "rockstar" culture)
- Having a ringer on your phone (because this is a musical instrument of *Shaytaan*)
- A woman sitting in front of a camera if the filmmaker is male (because he's forced to look directly through the lens at a non-*mahram* woman)
- Dancing, even in the privacy of your home (imitation of the *kuffaar* and wasting time)
- Dancing in front of your husband (because it will make him think you are an improper woman)
- Tying your hair or under-scarf into a bun (because it's a sign of the Day of Judgment about camel humps on your head)
- Writing poetry (wasting time)
- A woman going to Hajj or 'Umrah when she has no Muslim male relative (because it's *haraam* for a woman to travel without a *mahram*)
- A woman working outside the home (because her place is in the home)
- Working in a workplace where there are both men and women (because this is intermingling)
- A woman doing a radio interview (because men will hear her voice, which can be a sexual *fitnah*)

- Having a slit in your *niqaab* that exposes your eyes so you can see where you're going (because your eyes are a *fitnah* for men)
- A woman uncovering her face during Hajj or 'Umrah (because the men there will get distracted from their worship, as she is a sexual *fitnah*)
- Visiting non-Muslim relatives during the holidays, even if you do not participate in their celebrations or enter their houses of worship
- Attending an event or entering a place where there is music playing, even if it's your parents' house, a family wedding, or the store
- Going to a restaurant where alcohol is on the menu, even if you do not buy it yourself (because you should not be seated in a place where alcohol is served)
- Moving your fingers, hand or body rhythmically (or to a beat), even if in the privacy of your home (because *Shaytaan* is making you do this)
- A woman having money of her own without her husband's knowledge (because you have to get his permission for everything)
- A woman having a profile picture online or even in her passport (because a man might see it and get attracted to her)
- A man having a profile picture (because this is arrogance or violating the rules of *tasweer*)
- Having a photo album in your house (because it violates the rules of *tasweer*)
- A woman wearing nice or fashionable clothes, even if fully covered (because this is being ostentatious and thus violating the rules of hijab)
- An all-women fashion show (because it's a waste of time and "silly")
- A bridal shower (imitation of the *kuffaar*)
- A woman wearing anything that a man finds beautiful (because this is *zeenah*, even if her clothes are plain and not extravagant)
- Comedy (because it allegedly involves lying while joking)
- A woman riding in a taxi or car with an unrelated man driving (because you two are "alone")
- A woman wearing colors other than black (because it is *zeenah* and a *fitnah* for men)
- A woman having trim or designs on her *khimaar* or abaya (because it's *zeenah* and a *fitnah* for men)
- Leaving the Qur'an open if you're not reading it (because it's disrespecting the Qur'an)
- Hanging a Qur'an verse hanging on the wall (because it's disrespecting the Qur'an)
- A woman wearing heels (because it's lying about her height)
- Not committing to a single *madhhab* or school of thought (because this is considered religious misguidance, arrogance, or following your desires)

- Drinking or eating while standing
- A woman eating in a restaurant without a *mahram*
- A woman praying without socks
- A man praying in pants (because it shows his *'awrah*)
- A woman's voice on the answering machine or voicemail (because it's immodest and a *fitnah* for men who call)
- An unmarried man and woman speaking on the phone (because they are "alone")
- Following more than one *madhhab* opinion at a time (because it's not allowed to follow the Prophet, *peace be upon him*, from more than one scholarly source)
- Having more than one religious teacher (because it leads to confusion about Islam)
- Having an opinion that differs from the majority of scholars, even if the minority view is backed by Qur'an and Sunnah proofs and is recognized as valid by all scholars
- Disagreeing with *any* scholar, even if you naturally agree with another scholar on the same issue (because you're disrespecting the first one)
- Not doing *taqleed* (blind following) of a scholar (because this is religious arrogance)
- Not committing to a single religious sect or group (because this is following your desires and creating your own Islam)
- Striving to follow "only" the Qur'an and Sunnah (because this is religious misguidance or is virtually impossible, so you shouldn't even try)
- Doing calligraphy (can't remember why)
- Playing card games (imitating gambling)
- Playing board games (wasting time)
- Children acting in a school play (because this involves lying)
- Acting (because this involves lying)
- Clapping your hands in applause or at all (imitation of the *kuffaar* and because the Qur'an mentions disbelievers whistling and clapping their hands in worship)
- Killing a spider (because a spider is reported to have made a web to protect the Prophet, peace be upon him, in the cave)
- Killing ants (because ants are discussed honorably in the Qur'an)
- Women praying in congregation with other women (because women shouldn't be praying in *jamaa'ah*)
- Playing video games (because it's a waste of time)
- Women wearing deodorant (because this is like wearing perfume in front of men)

- Wearing any shoes or clothes with the Nike symbol (because "Nike" is a religious symbol like the cross or crucifix)
- A woman *reciting* Qur'an while she's on her menses
- Wearing a shoulder abaya (because it shows your shape or because only one single sheet of fabric is allowed to cover a woman's body)
- Eating meat from the People of the Book (because we can't be sure they killed the meat correctly)
- Eating turkey on Thanksgiving Day, even with no intent to celebrate the holiday
- Voting in non-Muslim elections (because it involves supporting ruling by other than what Allah revealed)
- Being a lawyer or judge in the West (same reason)
- A Muslim involved in politics (same reason)
- Saying *"Bismillah"* before making *wudhoo'* as the Prophet commanded, if the sink is in the bathroom or near a toilet (because you're disrespecting Allah's name)
- Attending or delivering a *Jumu'ah khutbah* (Friday sermon) spoken in English or any other non-Arabic language (because the *khutbah* is part of a formal prayer and formal prayers can only be said in Arabic)
- Making *du'aa* (supplicating to God in informal prayer) in your native language if you are non-Arab (because speaking to Allah or asking something of Him can only be done in Arabic)
- Using anything other than your fingers to enumerate your daily *dhikr* (remembrance of Allah)
- Using a prayer mat while praying (because this is allegedly against the Sunnah)
- Having any designs on the walls of the masjid (because beautifying the places of worship is *haraam*)
- Writing your name on the *outside of* the Qur'an you own so that everyone knows it belongs to you (because it's disrespecting the Qur'an)
- Using a pencil to write on the pages of the Qur'an to help with your memorization or recitation (because it's disrespecting the Qur'an)
- Singing a song written by non-Muslims, even for women at a women-only event for Eid or a wedding (because non-Muslim songs are evil and don't involve the remembrance of God)
- Singing a song about God written by a non-Muslim (because only Muslims can mention God in a respectable way)
- Saying "Eid Mubarak" or "Ramadan Mubarak" (because this is *bid'ah*, blameworthy religious innovation)
- Buying or exchanging gifts on Eid (imitation of the *kuffaar* and *bid'ah*)
- Decorating your house during Eid (imitation of the *kuffaar* and *bid'ah*)

- Having Arabic words hanging in the bathroom, even without Allah's name (because it's disrespecting the language of the Qur'an and Sunnah)
- Getting your ears or nose pierced (because it's harming your body or imitating the *kuffaar*)
- Getting braces (because it's changing the creation of Allah)
- Wearing color eye contacts (because it involves deceiving people)
- A woman owning and running an all-women hair and beauty salon (can't remember why)
- Using birth control or contraception (can't remember why)

And the list goes on…

How I Reclaimed My Faith

"Of the most doubtful matters to me is continuously staying away from what is doubtful to someone else because they said it should *be doubtful to me. This sort of spiritual manipulation makes me more fearful of my soul than that 'doubtful matter' ever could. So I stay away from doubtful by focusing on what my Lord has made clear—and by striving to* not *stress over others' never-ending 'what ifs' of mind and heart, which they label 'doubtful matters' in my faith."*
—from the journal of Umm Zakiyyah

By Allah's mercy, my spiritual insecurity never reached the point where I believed every single thing I heard labeled as "doubtful" in Islam. Thus, there are many things on that long list of doubtful that inspired more humor than genuine concern. Nevertheless, there were things that I gave up that I don't think I would have had I known what it would ultimately do to my *emaan*.

Prophet Muhammad (peace be upon him) said, "The Religion is easy. So whoever overburdens himself in his religion will not be able to continue in that way. So you should not go to extremes, rather strive to be near perfection. Receive good tidings that you will be rewarded, and gain strength by offering the prayers in the mornings, afternoons, and during the last hours of the nights" (Bukhari).

As I reflected on the burdens I'd put on myself and the personal extremes to which I'd gone to "be safe," I had an epiphany: Religious safety isn't an objective matter; it's a personal matter. Safety isn't something you arrive at based on a theoretical reality "out there"… on the pages of Islamic books or in scholarly lectures. It's something you arrive at based on your spiritual reality "in here"... in the heart and soul—and rooted in what you truly understand and believe about your faith.

No, you certainly cannot throw out objectivity altogether and ignore scholarly evidences, but after steering clear of what is undeniably wrong and doing what is undeniably obligatory, religious safety is first and foremost what preserves your soul.

What 'Staying Away From Doubtful' Really Means

It is well known that religion is defined by core beliefs and specific acts of worship. Islam is no different. Thus, the rules of what we believe and how we worship are very specific. In fact, they form the very definition of faith. The slightest deviation from what Allah and His Messenger taught regarding belief and worship is at the very least *bid'ah* (blameful religious innovation) and at the worst *kufr* (disbelief in Islam itself). **Hence, our greatest concern for religious safety must be in protecting our beliefs and worship.**

It is well known that worldly affairs, as a general rule, are not religious matters. Thus, humans are free to enjoy and benefit from anything of this world that they wish—unless Allah has expressly forbidden it (i.e. eating pork, drinking alcohol, or engaging in any sexual intimacy outside the God-mandated union between a man and a woman).

In other words, all matters of belief and worship have the general principle of prohibition unless there is clear proof for them in the Qur'an and Sunnah; and all matters related to our worldly life have the general principle of permissibility unless there is clear proof against them in the Qur'an and Sunnah.

Thus, for me, I was able to reclaim my faith by staying away from doubtful by adhering to this general rule, rooted in the Qur'an and Sunnah: *If I hear of a religious belief or mode of worship that I cannot be absolutely sure (based on evidences) is sanctioned in the Qur'an or the Sunnah, I stay away from it "to be safe." But if I hear of a worldly matter being prohibited based on "proofs" not rooted in clear evidences from the Qur'an and Sunnah (or historical* ijmaa'), *I consider it permissible "to be safe."*

Focus on Allah, Not Other People's Doubts

Reaching a spiritual place where I could let go of other people's doubts and focus on my own has been a long, tough road. Shedding the indoctrination that I don't have a right to my own mind, life, and soul has not been easy, as many communities and Islamic classes don't teach *tawakkul*, such that you establish a personal relationship with Allah and trust in Him alone. They teach human dependency and scholar-worship, such that you establish a spiritual relationship with your imam or teacher, whom you are expected to trust to do your thinking and soul-work on your behalf.

In some cultures, this human dependency is taught as being between parent and child, such that parents must be trusted to do the thinking and soul-work on the children's behalf, even when these "children" are now adults.

However, in my own spiritual crisis, I reached a point where this "so-and-so always knows better than you" thinking was no longer an option, literally. It was either let go of this human dependency or let go of my *emaan*. I chose my *emaan*.

Today, I consciously stay away from environments and classes that teach self-denial over self-care, particularly regarding worldly matters subject to permissible disagreement. Islam itself has enough rules and guidelines that restrict aspects of our worldly life such that healthy self-denial is an integral part of practicing our faith. Thus, I don't understand the obsession of some Muslims with continuously adding to this list.

And here, I differentiate between those who follow the strictest view because they genuinely believe it to be correct in front of Allah (and thus respectfully share with others what they've studied or learned), and those who resort to emotional manipulation or spiritual abuse when it becomes clear that the other person is not convinced that such-and-such is *haraam*. When their threats of Hellfire, censuring quotes from their sheikhs, and implications that the person is a bad Muslim don't work; like clockwork, they resort to the final spiritual manipulation technique, as if reciting from a memorized script: "You should stay away from what's doubtful."

Today, when I hear this statement used as a guilt tactic to convince someone to follow the strictest view on a non-*ijmaa'* issue, I sometimes have to recite *dhikr* to calm down, I get so angry. As I mentioned in my blog "Suffering From Religious OCD?": You cannot live your entire life throwing every worldly issue into the category of "doubtful matters" just because you aren't personally aware of its specific "ruling" in Islam. If you do, you'll likely overburden yourself in the religion until you are paralyzed into inactivity, anxiety, and stress—and until you give up on practicing Islam altogether.

Furthermore, as many scholars have explained, "doubtful matters" is not a definitive category of issues in Islam. What is doubtful to one person is not doubtful to another, as "doubtful" depends on each individual person's level of Islamic knowledge, as well as his or her own internal discomfort with something.

Unfortunately, it is rare that a Muslim advises a fellow believer to simply turn to Allah for guidance on how to handle a practical dilemma or a confusing predicament that involves permissible disagreement in Islam. Instead, we rush to make the person's life difficult by saying, "Stay away from doubtful," as if this is the cure-all to all of life's problems and uncertainties. But we label this approach "protecting the soul."

However, I know firsthand the spiritual harms of continuous self-denial in the name of "protecting your soul." I stayed away from any and every thing that I felt could even be *possibly* be doubtful, only to find myself exhausted and my soul harmed so much that I felt I couldn't even be Muslim anymore. I wish it had occurred to me that the most serious "doubtful matter" to stay away from is that which makes me doubt my faith itself.

Allah says what has been translated to mean:

> **"And they were not commanded except to worship Allah, [being] sincere to Him in religion, inclining to truth, and to establish prayer and to give *zakaah*. And that is the correct religion."**
> —*Al-Bayyinah* (98:5)

5
What If You're Wrong?

◆

"The constant micromanagement of our thoughts and life choices, even down to how we move our head or finger as we hum a song to ourselves, has led so many of us to near nervous breakdowns. The concept of 'commanding the good and forbidding the evil' has become, in so many Muslim communities, merely a euphemism for 'license to abuse and harm.'"
—from the journal of Umm Zakiyyah

When I, along with a small group of artists and Muslim scholars, decided to speak up against the slander and verbal abuse continuously aimed at Muslims who do not view all music as *haraam*, I was told that the honor and reputation of Muslims involved in music should be sacrificed in the interest of never "disrespecting" the Islamic scholars who slander them. As harsh as these words look in print, this is precisely what I was told.

For the record, when speaking against the slander and verbal abuse, the group mentioned not a single scholar's name, as the focus was on the troubling issue, not on any specific people—and it certainly was not only scholars who were guilty of this wrongdoing. Fortunately, the forum we planned to address this egregious problem was a success and gained support from many Islamic scholars themselves, including those who viewed all music as *haraam*.

Yet still, to many other "practicing Muslims," the honor and reputation of a person who listened to music meant nothing, so these "music people" should accept all the verbal abuse directed at them, even when they are effectively being labeled disbelievers. In other words, I was told that it is an Islamic duty of believers who listen to music to accept being accused of having no love of Allah or Qur'an in their hearts, to accept being labeled homosexuals, and to accept being categorized as agents of *Shaytaan*—specifically when these calumnies are spoken on the tongue of someone with a scholarly title.

Unfortunately, this insanity under the guise of "commanding the good and forbidding the evil" and "respecting scholars" has become normalized in many Muslim communities that claim to be following the Sunnah. It is so common in fact that I have come to see it as the normalized extremism of our modern times. While it is certainly a form of religious misguidance for Muslims to become extremely lax in their religion when they seek to "normalize" Islam for our times, it is also a form of religious misguidance for Muslims become so strict in their religion that they seek to normalize extremism during our times.

We can talk about the strong evidences supporting the view that all music is *haraam* (except the *daff*), and we can talk about the "weak" evidences supporting the view that the restrictions on music are not limited to only the *daff*. However, no matter what conclusion we come to, nothing justifies slandering believers and denying the love of Allah or Qur'an in their hearts.

At worst, concerning this non-*ijmaa'* issue, the Muslim has fallen into error by following the incorrect opinion (whichever that is); and at best, the Muslim is doing what he or she sincerely understands to be correct in front of Allah—even if we don't understand why or how. Nevertheless, even if they are mistaken, their error is not a sin; it is not *bid'ah*; and it is not *kufr* or *shirk*. And we have no right to slander them.

What Is Really Going On Here?

When I first began studying about Islam and stopped listening to music myself, Muslims in the community I was part of at the time ostracized me and called me crazy. So I know firsthand how it feels to be punished for being on the "wrong side" of permissible scholarly disagreement. However, at the time, I couldn't fathom what my friends and community members were so up in arms about.

After becoming part of another Muslim community and witnessing the same uproar directed at those who listened to music, I became curious as to why, out of all the controversial issues today, music is such a hot button—so much so that many Muslims are unable to discuss it without becoming visibly irate, and inconsolably so. And here, I'm not speaking only about those who believe music is *haraam*. I'm speaking also about those who insist that it is permitted.

Today, I don't claim to understand all the dynamics in play that makes music such an emotional topic, but I have come to understand better the charged emotions on both sides. In my studies and experience, I can pinpoint some phenomena that account for at least some of the excessive emotionalism on both sides.

For those who believe music is *haraam* and have difficulty remaining levelheaded when faced with someone who believes it is allowed, they are generally responding to at least one of three realities (if not all):

1. They were taught that the prohibition of music is a clear, *ijmaa'* issue similar to the prohibition of alcohol, adultery, and homosexual acts. In other words, for whatever reason, their religious classes exaggerated the Islamic evidences surrounding music such that the historical majority opinion was portrayed as the "only opinion." Thus, the minority view (which was historically viewed as only "weak" by those who disagreed with it) was now understood as an invention of modern times, and thus clear *bid'ah* or *kufr* (since the absence of

historical *ikhtilaaf* implies the intentional changing of *haraam* to *halaal*).
2. They equate the acceptance of music with the acceptance of "Western culture" or imitation of the *kuffaar* and thus the dismantling of their own cultures or of "Islamic culture" itself. (This association is common amongst colonized regions in the Muslim world and amongst Muslim immigrants to the West who wish to preserve some semblance of their home cultures while gaining Western citizenship).
3. Music is utilized as an act of worship in some sects of Islam. In these sects, reciting sacred chants and dancing and twirling to music are viewed as acceptable (and praiseworthy) means to draw close to Allah, and these activities sometimes replace prayer and prophetic *dhikr* itself. (This perhaps explains the widespread view that love of music and love of Qur'an or Allah cannot exist in the same heart. Perhaps, the scholars who initially made this observation were discussing music that is used, literally, as a replacement for prayer, authentic *dhikr*, and reciting Qur'an. And Allah knows best)

For those who believe that the prophetic restrictions on music do not rule all music as *haraam*, yet they have difficulty remaining levelheaded when faced with someone who believes music is *haraam*, are generally responding to at least one of three realities (if not all):
1. They were taught that the prohibition of music is rooted in the teachings of misguided religious extremists.
2. They are responding to the continuous equation of their cultural practices and religious views with "imitation of the *kuffaar*" or spiritual corruption. Also, amongst African-Americans who view music as permissible, they are responding to the consistent subtle and blatant anti-Black racism often taught under the umbrella of "the harms of viewing music as allowed."
3. If they are part of the sects of Islam that utilize music as worship, they are exasperated that someone could label as *haraam* something that is (according to their sect) a means to draw closer to Allah.

Lying for the Sake of Allah?

I mention music here because being in both hostile environments—amongst those who went to extremes in saying music is allowed, and those who went to extremes in saying music is *haraam*—contributed significantly to my own ultimate spiritual exhaustion. I often felt as if there was no emotional safety in any Muslim community. You either followed the prevailing point of view on music and slandered those who didn't, or you risked being slandered yourself. I couldn't understood what was so hard about accepting that a Muslim could be sincere and beloved to Allah while viewing music as *haraam*, and a Muslim could be sincere and beloved to Allah while viewing music as allowed.

Even if a person was wrong and thus in need of Allah's mercy and forgiveness, how was he or she different from any other flawed believer, as we are *all* in need of Allah's mercy and forgiveness. No one can get *everything* right. So what's the problem?

During my initial formal studies of Islam, I myself was taught that the prohibition of music was an issue of historical *ijmaa'*, so I naturally stayed away from it completely. When I continued my studies of Islam for many years and eventually learned that this initial teaching was an exaggeration of truth, I began to question so many other things I had been taught.

When I began to ask more questions regarding why certain things were taught as inflexible truths instead of historical *ikhtilaaf* (even if most scholars viewed the opinion as "weak"), I was told that it is necessary for scholars to "block the path to evil." In other words, in the interest of saving the *ummah* for corruption, full disclosure of truth is not always necessary or wise.

This confounded me. I understood teaching Islam according to spiritual priorities and thus not overwhelming new Muslims or new learners with long lists of do's and don'ts. But I didn't understand lying. There is a huge difference between focusing on the most crucial matters while saving other issues for later, and flat out saying that historically there is no other valid or permissible view on a matter except the one being taught.

What's Your Definition of Evil?

Because my own Islamic studies were motivated by a desire to learn what was true and stay away from falsehood (as opposed to joining a specific group or studying under a specific teacher), I have no words for the sense of betrayal I felt when I learned, one after the other, the "necessary lies" being taught in many Muslim groups under the umbrella of "blocking the path to evil."

Those who insisted that laypeople had to blindly follow scholars were "blocking the path to evil." Those who insisted that *taqleed* of a specific *madhhab* was obligatory were "blocking the path to evil." Those who insisted that women must cover their eyes (even though it wasn't required in Islam) were "blocking the path to evil." Those who said abused women should stay with their husbands were "blocking the path to evil." Those who said polygamy wasn't allowed in modern times (or for those living in the West) were "blocking the path to evil." And on and on, Muslims presented one permissible point of view—or outright fabrications—as Islam itself, in the interest of some "greater good" and blocking some evil that they had imagined for the *ummah*.

Upon hearing this, all I could think was, if lying about our faith (and denying believers the right to make informed decisions based on all facts) isn't evil, what is *your* definition of evil?

What If You're Wrong?

Needless to say, this experience only reinforced my determination to heed the prophetic advice to guard myself against religious sectarianism: *Isolate yourself from all of these sects, even if you have to eat the roots of trees until death overcomes you while you are in that state.*

However, what was I supposed to do? If I couldn't trust what I was being taught in most Islamic classes regarding permissible disagreement, how would I learn what view was right? What if I follow the wrong point of view and end up in Hellfire? What could I possibly do to protect myself?

How I Reclaimed My Faith

*"Islam is not about always being right.
It's about remaining on the right path."*
—from the journal of Umm Zakiyyah

After my paranoia calmed somewhat, I began to see the blessing in all of my confusion and uncertainty. What I had previously imagined to be a spiritual catastrophe was merely a powerful lesson in the true meaning of *emaan* and *tawakkul*. By being placed in a predicament where I was repeatedly faced with controversial issues and no tangible guarantee that I was following the right point of view, I was forced to examine my heart and intentions in a way that I never had before. I was also forced to connect with my Lord in a way I never had before.

In my honest self-examination, I realized for the first time the spiritual harm that can come from always following the "safest" opinion or from attaching yourself to a spiritual teacher who always made these decisions for you. In both cases, the possibility of being "wrong" (and thus accountable) was largely removed, even if only in our logic or imagination. In this odd logic, we view our "safe" choices as removing ourselves from even *needing* Allah's mercy and forgiveness for what we do. Thus, we subconsciously assume we are always spiritually safe or right—whether due to following the strictest point of view or to blindly trusting a "person of knowledge." However, what we don't realize is that in this "safe" spiritual environment—which ostensibly removes the likelihood of falling into sin or doubt—the seeds of pride are planted, as they now have both fertile ground and daily cultivation.

To look at it from another angle: Being aware of the consistent likelihood of having fallen into sin or spiritual danger humbles the believing heart and cultivates a healthy fear of Allah. It also stills the tongue from speaking with confidence about the rightness of what one is doing. Without being aware of the consistent likelihood of having fallen into sin or spiritual danger, the heart is more susceptible to feeling both sin-free and guilt-free, feelings that feed pride and self-satisfaction, which in turn lessen the likelihood of feeling natural fear of Allah. Moreover, when we feel sin-free and guilt-free, we are less likely to still our tongues from speaking with confidence about the rightness of what we're doing—and the necessity of others living as we are.

Ironically, in reality, even when we are following the "safest" point of view and blindly trusting "people of knowledge," we are still potentially in sin and spiritual danger. However, our imagination that we are doing what is "safest" and "staying away from doubt" blocks us from being conscious of our potential sin and spiritual danger. Thus, feeling the urgency to repent for our potential wrongs is less likely than the one who is conscious of their potential sin and spiritual danger.

To illustrate, let's look at a rather common example: It is no less dangerous to label the *halaal* as *haraam* than it is to label the *haraam* as *halaal*. Likewise, it is no less a grave sin to teach Muslims that the *halaal* is *haraam* than it is to teach them that the *haraam* is *halaal*. However, many practicing Muslims who view themselves as religious are generally fearful of permitting what could be forbidden by Allah, but they don't exercise the same caution when forbidding what could be permitted by Allah. Yet both are serious sins. Why the discrepancy?

For whatever reason, many of them believe that it is somehow praiseworthy to potentially change Allah's religion to be stricter than it is in reality; and they believe that is blameworthy to potentially change Allah's religion to be more lenient than it is in reality. Consequently, they imagine that they gain blessings for the former and sin for the latter. Thus, they feel sin-free and guilt-free while following the strictest point of view, but they feel sinful and guilt-ridden while following the more lenient point of view.

However, in Islam, determining truth and falsehood on a controversial issue is based on the strength of the Islamic evidences, not on the strictness of the point of view. Sometimes the strictest point of view has the strongest evidences, and sometimes it has the weakest. Similarly, sometimes the lenient point of view has the strongest evidences, and sometimes it has the weakest. Thus, the closest we can get to religious safety when faced with unclear matters is striving to follow the point of view that is most strongly supported by Islamic evidences—while understanding that there is always the possibility that we could be wrong or mistaken, irrespective of the strictness or leniency of the view.

Most seriously, the terms *halaal* and *haraam* should never be used lightly, as using these terms represent speaking on behalf of Allah. While there are definitely foundational and clear matters that *require* our use of these terms (lest we fall into sin by denying the Words of Allah), there is an etiquette that must be observed when using these terms in discussions of permissible disagreement.

The necessity of caution in using the terms *halaal* and *haraam* is why, historically, the scholars of the Sunnah generally discuss controversial issues in terms of what position has the "strongest evidences" as opposed to what is definitely *halaal* and *haraam*. When they use the terms *halaal* and *haraam* in discussions of permissible disagreement, they often preface their statements with phrases such as, "It is the view of such-and-such scholar (or school of thought) that *xyz* is allowed (or forbidden)" or "It is our view that..." And they generally end these discussions with the statement, "And Allah knows best." Furthermore, when they discuss the scholars (or believers) who disagree with them, they generally say the person is "mistaken" or that the view is "weak" or incorrect. However, they make no pronouncements about the state of these believers' souls or their affair in front of Allah.

Interestingly, this is in sharp contrast to how most laypeople, and even some scholars of today, treat controversial issues and those believers with a different point of view, hence the normalized extremism on both sides of the music controversy.

Uncertainty Is Healthy for the Soul

As I was examining my own heart and soul after my initial paranoia subsided, I realized that I had mistakenly equated *uncertainty* with *doubt*, which largely contributed to my spiritual exhaustion. In other words, I had assumed that being unable to know something with certainty was the same as dealing with an issue that fell under *mushtabihaat*, as discussed in the hadith:

> "The *halaal* (permissible) is clear and the *haraam* (forbidden) is clear, and between them are matters that are *mushtabihaat* [unclear or doubtful]. Whoever is wary of these doubtful matters has absolved his religion and honor. And whoever indulges in them has indulged in the *haraam*. It is like a shepherd who herds his sheep too close to preserved sanctuary, and they will eventually graze in it. Every king has a sanctuary, and the sanctuary of Allah is what He has made *haraam*..." (Bukhari and Muslim).

In reality, the only issues that involved absolutely no possibility of uncertainty were foundational and clear matters that were not subject to legitimate scholarly disagreement in the first place. Any issues that were not foundational, clear, or *ijmaa'* (by definition) involved *some* level of uncertainty. However, religious safety and avoiding doubt was achieved by striving our level best to adhere to the view most strongly supported by the evidences in the Qur'an and Sunnah.

Doubtful matters, however, as I learned during my Islamic studies, varied from person to person based on their level of knowledge and understanding. Therefore, these "doubtful" issues could not possibly be a solid category in Islam because "the *halaal* is clear and the *haraam* is clear," and to categorize doubtful as a definitive category would be contradicting the hadith itself. Thus, what was required of each believer was to strive their level best to learn their religion, such that the *halaal* and *haraam* became clear. If for any reason a particular issue disturbed a person's heart (whether due to ignorance or due to it remaining doubtful even after being presented with evidences), generally, the safest route was to avoid it.

In contrast, having a level of uncertainty regarding non-foundational issues was the natural result of being ever aware of one's human fallibility and the possibility of falling into error, even when the heart itself is not doubtful or disturbed by the matter. This level of humility in front of Allah is what I am referring to when I say uncertainty is good for the soul.

Your Heart Will Reveal You To You

You can only lie to yourself but for so long, before your heart cries out and demands to bear witness. I penned these words in my journal as I reflected pensively on the spiritual trials that I was going through, and what they had exposed of my heart. In reflecting on these trials, I find it quite profound that the Prophet (peace be upon him) ended the discussion of doubtful matters with this statement about the human heart: *If it is sound, the whole body is sound; and if it is corrupted, the whole body is corrupted.*

During this difficult time, I had come to realize that much of what I had imagined as "religious safety" was merely a manifestation of unhealthy self-doubt and lack of *tawakkul* in Allah. I cannot speak for anyone else who has gone through spiritual crisis, but I know for myself, I uncovered a lot of buried toxic shame that was linked more to unhealed emotional wounds than to my being sincerely convinced that following the strictest view was always most pleasing to Allah. I also realized that much of my strictness was linked to my feeling that I didn't have the right to exist and that I was an inherently bad, corrupt person. My strictness allowed me to never have to face myself in that I never "gave my Lord a reason" to put me in Hell, though I felt I belonged there.

Safety Is Awareness of Danger, Not the Absence of the Danger

Safety lies in being ever aware of the spiritual danger you are potentially in, not in the absence of being exposed to spiritual danger itself. For this reason, we should never feel completely "safe" no matter what point of view we follow in scholarly disagreement.

It is relevant to note here that following the strictest scholarly view can indeed be safest for our souls when it does not lead to overburdening ourselves, or to speaking on behalf of Allah regarding what is definitely forbidden. Similarly, consistently trusting a particular scholar or sheikh can indeed be safest for our souls when it does not lead to neglecting our individual obligations to Allah and self-care, or to speaking on behalf of Allah regarding how other Muslims should view our favored scholar or sheikh.

For there is a huge difference between following the strictest view out of fear of Allah, and teaching that it is the only valid or correct point of view in Islam. Likewise, there is a huge difference between following a scholar you trust because you genuinely believe he is most knowledgeable in certain matters, and insisting that others are obligated to trust and follow him like you do.

In other words, while seeking religious safety in our actions, we should not carelessly throw ourselves into spiritual danger with our tongues.

The Link Between Conviction and Cruelty

As I engaged in painful self-honesty, I began to see the blessing in battling this spiritual crisis instead of becoming "safer" and "safer" in my Islamic practice. I began to realize that my suffering was protecting me from overburdening myself in my faith and from falling into the self-deception that is often fueled by unhealthy conviction.

While conviction is both healthy and necessary when it is rooted in fundamental, unquestionable truths about Allah and Islam, it becomes unhealthy and toxic when it removes the fear of Allah from our hearts, especially when speaking about how others should practice the faith. As I mentioned, religious safety in our actions should never equal carelessness with our tongues. When it does, it is not religious safety we are engaged in, but self-deception and destructive pride.

Realizing this made me understand why I was unable to feel emotionally safe around many Muslims. Those who incited in me the most mental distress and emotional turmoil were often deeply involved in religious groups or circles that had one of two traits: They were generally following the strictest point of view on most controversial matters, or they were aligned with a specific imam, scholar, or sheikh whom they generally followed without question.

In both cases, the possibility of being wrong or accountable was largely removed (at least consciously) from them. Thus, they felt both sin-free and guilt free in nearly everything they did. This in turn cultivated pride in their hearts and lack of caution in their speech and behavior. And because they consistently believed they were on the side of God in their points of view—either because it was the "safest" or because a "person of knowledge" said so—there was no need to consider the possibility of being wrong or the need to show humility, mercy, or empathy when speaking to others.

In their minds, being harsh to "the people of desires" or denying the *emaan* of the "rejecters of scholars" was necessary to stop this corruption from infecting the rest of the *ummah*. In other words, these Muslims' lack of fear of Allah regarding their tongues—due to unhealthy conviction and unchecked pride—was viewed as a manifestation of fear of Allah itself.

This realization terrified me. *O Allah, protect me from myself!* I prayed.

But What If You're Wrong?

As I asked myself this question, some others came to mind: What if those who consistently followed the strictest opinion entertained the very real possibility that *their* point of view was wrong in front of Allah? What if they also considered the grave sin of making the *halaal haraam* whenever they spoke with certainty about such-and-such being *haraam*? What if they felt the need to humbly say, "Allah knows best" when they shared their perspective instead of condemning to Hell those who disagreed with them?

This pause, this simple pause—inspired by healthy uncertainty—cultivates a humble heart that is fearful of Allah and a tongue that hesitates to speak on behalf of one's Lord, whether one is following a "strict" or "lenient" point of view.

For surely, when one's heart is ever mindful of Allah, irrespective of the apparent "safety" of one's outward actions, then the tongue and body follow in humility and good character: "…There lies within the body a piece of flesh. If it is sound, the whole body is sound; and if it is corrupted, the whole body is corrupted. Verily, it is the heart" (Bukhari and Muslim).

Regarding the ever-present possibility of being wrong even as we continuously strive to please our Lord, Allah says:

> **"Say, O My slaves who have wronged their souls!**
> **Despair not of the mercy of Allah. Verily, Allah forgives all sins.**
> **Truly, He is Oft-Forgiving, Most Merciful."**
> —*Az-Zumar* (39:53)

6

I Stayed Away From People

"Sometimes you just have to accept that you no longer share any significant common ground with people you once knew, no matter how close you used to be or how much you once benefited from them. So it's time to let go and move on."
—from the journal of Umm Zakiyyah

If there is anything these last few years have taught me, it is that no one is coming to your aid—except Allah Himself—and that no one truly cares about you, except a select few believers. And they're often not the people you expected to be there for you.

Don't get me wrong. I don't think that our friends and loved ones or our brothers and sisters in faith sit around intending to hurt and abandon us. It's something they do naturally, often without even realizing it. And that's what scares me. Because I'm human too, so I imagine I must do it myself without knowing it. May Allah forgive us and help us, and remove these spiritual diseases from our hearts.

But there is some hurt and abandonment that is not merely an honest mistake or a sincere oversight. It is the result of a culture of abuse put in place by a system of religious elitism. And here, I use the term *religious elitism* to refer to the use of religion as a means to establish a spiritual hierarchy. In this hierarchy, sincere worshippers are indoctrinated into believing that there are people who matter and people who don't—and the former are usually the religious leaders and the latter are "the commoners." However, when these systems of religious elitism favor cultures of people with their own systems of discrimination and mistreatment (racism, misogyny, domestic violence, sexual abuse, child abuse, etc.), the problem is exacerbated beyond measurement or comprehension.

Naturally, the details of each system of religious elitism varies from culture to culture and group to group, but nearly all of them have at least one of these five characteristics (and some have all):

1. **They do not honor or accept the God-given right of each individual to self-care and soul-preservation**, specifically when the elite are insisting that the "lowly person" heeds their demands. In other words, as I discussed earlier, they view it as an affront and a sin to

honor the maxim that represents the dividing line between respect and abuse, freedom and tyranny, and human rights and oppression: *Whenever you genuinely believe that serving, pleasing, or obeying someone will displease God or harm your life and soul, honor your life and soul.*

2. **They silence and criminalize permissible disagreement.** In other words, they have beliefs and behavior codes that are not obligatory in Islam, but they present them as if they are. Thus, if anyone disagrees with their view or follows another permissible view, they use emotional manipulation or spiritual abuse to convince the person that they are wrong. If this doesn't work, they resort to slander, ostracizing, name-calling, or character assassination to convince others that God is displeased with the person. They sometimes go as far as to incite group members against the "dissenter."

3. **They punish those who find fault in them or who speak up against any abuse**, as "dissenters" are viewed as threats to the elitist system. In this aspect of religious elitism, the sins and wrongs of the elite are defended or trivialized, and anyone who speaks up after being wronged is labeled a "bad Muslim" or is accused of disobeying or displeasing God. If the elite are forced to address the wrong because it is publicized or widespread, they continuously highlight all the good the wrongdoer has done while trivializing or denying the wrongdoing itself. In this, they literally "play God," declaring that the wrongdoer's good outweighs the bad and that the crime committed is nothing compared to all of his good. In this way, the wronged are punished and humiliated while being portrayed as sinful troublemakers who wish to tarnish the pristine image (or challenge the lofty spiritual station) of the religious elite.

4. **They slander those who do not follow them,** as these non-members are also threats to the elitist system. Depending on the group or culture, this slander is done either overtly or covertly, but the slander is generally taught as if it is part of Islam itself. Here is where labels and name-calling are most effective. These elite groups generally use praiseworthy labels for themselves and offensive labels for others, thereby detracting the layperson's focus from distinguishing spiritual truth from spiritual falsehood—and thus eliminating the possibility of the elite being questioned or accountable when wrong. Those who have been indoctrinated into these groups tend to trust Muslims who carry their group's label and distrust those who don't, even without fully understanding their own group's actual beliefs or the beliefs of "the other."

5. **They require blind obedience and complete allegiance.** To achieve this, the layperson's indoctrination begins very early on, such that their first "Islamic lessons" are about their inability to understand Islam without the help and assistance of a spiritual teacher, thus necessitating *taqleed* (blind following) of a religious authority or a singe school of thought (which often bears little resemblance to the original school of thought carrying the same name). This guarantees that the layperson will consistently equate pleasing Allah with obeying the spiritual leader.

I reflect on this phenomenon in my journal: *It is no coincidence that the first lesson given to new members of most religious groups is* taqleed *(blind following), to establish complete dependence on a single spiritual teacher—as opposed to* Tawheed *(Oneness of Allah), to establish a complete dependence on Allah alone. The former ensures that guidance is forever connected to your relationship to a specific human being, whereas the latter ensures that guidance is forever connected to your relationship with the Creator.*

Regarding these abusive, mind-controlling elitist systems, I also wrote this in my journal:

The Prophet (peace be upon him) was sent to free us from the shackles of worshipping men to the freedom of worshipping the Creator. But some Muslims want to return us to the shackles of worshipping men while trying to convince us it's a requirement of worshipping the Creator.

But my Lord is Allah, and bi'idhnillaah, *I will not allow anyone to come between me and my soul, no matter what fancy label they put on their misguidance or invitation to* shirk—*and no matter how many "Islamic degrees" and years of study they claim to have that grants them the qualification to be called "sheikh", "scholar" or "spiritual teacher."*

*There is no lofty label or scholarly qualification that grants any human being the right to call to a spiritual path or religious teaching that is not directly from Prophet Muhammad (*sallallaahu'alayhi wa sallam*).*

If you have been granted the tremendous blessing of beneficial knowledge, then by all means, share it with the world. But do not seek to prop yourself up as an intermediary between the people and Allah, saying that religious allegiance to you (or your favored sheikh) equals religious allegiance to the Creator. That in itself is a sign that you do not have even basic *Islamic knowledge.*

I think it relevant to reiterate here something that I mentioned earlier regarding the necessity to guard ourselves from all invitations to the Hellfire, no matter where or whom it comes from:

> *Many who rejected the Messengers in history were resentful that the Prophet whom Allah sent to them did not have the qualities they felt made him honorable and worthy of such a noble role, whether it was wealth, power, or a certain lineage. And many who followed misguidance in history were pleased with the "noble" traits of the one leading them to Hellfire, whether it was because the inviter was a parent, a "righteous" person, or someone they deemed honorable in some worldly way.*
>
> *Today, we find history repeating itself in Muslims rejecting obvious spiritual truths because the person speaking the truth does not have a lofty scholarly title, did not study overseas or in an Islamic university, or is not part of our favored group, sect, or culture.*
>
> *Be careful.*
>
> *Many times Allah tests us by placing the truth on the tongue of one who will reveal to us the very depths of our hearts—and our response to this divine truth will make plain to us whether it is Allah or our pride that is most beloved to us in this world.*
>
> *O dear soul, be careful.*

While this warning is certainly relevant to laypeople who dismiss or trivialize the knowledge of scholars teaching authentic Islam, it is also very relevant to those who are scholars themselves but have fallen into error, whether due to natural human fallibility or to having studied in a system rooted in falsehood.

Undoubtedly, it is difficult to dedicate years of your life to something only to realize in a moment's clarification that you were wrong and that, for the sake of your soul, you need to tread a different path. Many converts to Islam understand this feeling on a deeply personal level, especially those who had been religious preachers or ministers in their former faith tradition. However, this predicament is not unique to non-Muslims. It happens to Muslims too, even those who are imams, scholars, sheikhs, or Islamic preachers.

Though we often hear the stories of laypeople who move from sect to sect and sheikh to sheikh in search of spiritual truth, it is rare you hear the stories of scholars and sheikhs themselves openly admitting that they were wrong and in need of repentance for spreading false teachings. Similarly, it is more common to hear stories of average people converting to Islam than of priests, ministers, or rabbis leaving their religions to become Muslim. However, following spiritual truth is no less obligatory upon religious scholars than it is upon common people. Why then is there such a wide discrepancy in who accepts truth?

The answer is so simple that it is chilling: The more we stand to lose in terms of our worldly status, earthly comforts, and pride, the less likely we are to follow the truth when it comes to us. However, given the nature of spiritual matters and the tests that Allah promises He will give us on earth, we can be almost one hundred percent certain that we will be asked to sacrifice one or all of these throughout our lives, sometimes repeatedly.

But will we be ready?

From 'Un-Mosqued' to Un-Peopled

In my fear of tying my heart and life to something that would harm my soul in some irrevocable way, I began to more and more distance myself from religious groups and communities. However, this was an extremely lonely experience, and I didn't like this life path. Like everyone else, I wanted companionship and a community to call my own, but nearly everywhere I went, there was some form of religious elitism in place.

Before my spiritual crisis, I was able to be patient with the elitism and focus on the benefits that I was gaining in certain social circles and Islamic classes. *O Allah, make me benefit from what is good and truthful, and protect me from what is harmful and false*, I consistently prayed. However, I was finding that my defenses were weakening, and I increasingly felt the need to "just belong." I was tired of having to filter so much of what I was learning.

The truth is, during this time, I didn't have to filter what I was learning any more than I normally would, as the necessity to filter what we learn from humans is a basic fact of life that cannot (and should not) be avoided, no matter whom and where we're learning from. Rather what was happening was that the unaddressed emotional wounds that I had suppressed for so long were beginning to implode, such that I was now exhibiting symptoms of complex PTSD (post traumatic stress disorder), specifically emotional triggers and heightened anxiety in the presence of others, especially environments that mirrored some aspects of the initial trauma.

From young, I had been taught that I did not have the right to exist and that my thoughts, life path, and soul had to be sacrificed in service of people and cultures that were more important and valuable than I was. These included parents, elders, family, husband, the African-American people, American democracy, and specific religious leaders who had been given the title imam, sheikh, scholar, or spiritual teacher.

In my accepting the assignment of my personal disappearance from existence, I was not allowed to consult my own mind, heart, or soul in pursuit of self-care or individual spirituality. If I ever sought these, I was reminded that God had commanded my self-sacrifice and that I was being "disrespectful" to those in authority over me by voicing my own "selfishness" and "arrogance."

Even if anyone "with authority over me" or from the "more important" groups harmed me in any way, I had to bear it in silence "for the greater good."

"Our people get enough bad press!" an African-American Muslim commented after I had posted a blog reflecting on what I had learned from being part of a small African-American community that ostracized and slandered me after I would not give complete blind allegiance to their imam or practice Islam in the way they approved. In other words, she was telling me what I had heard in nearly every community I was part of: *You don't matter. Our image does.*

This damaging message is sent to children of abuse who are tasked with protecting the family image. This message is sent to victims of domestic violence who are tasked with protecting the image of their husband or wife. This message is sent to church and synagogue congregants who suffered harm from religious leaders. And this message is sent to Muslim men and women who were wronged or abused by the religious elite.

When I attended Islamic classes, if I asked a single question that appeared to suggest even the *possibility* of having a point of view different from the community's religious elite, I was berated with, "Who do you think you are? He has way more knowledge than you!" In this way, the culture of the religous elite was reinforced by the indoctrinated followers, who were convinced that silencing their thoughts and feelings, even if only when asking a sincere question, was displeasing Allah or was a violation of Islamic *adab*.

Unfortunately, the combination of my inquisitive nature (as this is how I learn best) and the widespread culture of religious elitism made it impossible for me to sit in Islamic classes or even most social gatherings without being deeply triggered. I would often come home physically sick and unable to even walk or stand for prayer. My migraines increased and my health plummeted until I had to resign from my fulltime job and stay home until my body regained its strength to function properly.

How I Reclaimed My Faith

"None of you should wish for death due to a calamity that has afflicted him. Yet if he must do something, let him say, 'O Allah, keep me alive so long as life is good for me, and cause me to die if death is better for me.'"
—Prophet Muhammad, peace be upon him
(Sahih al-Bukhari 5347, Sahih Muslim 2680)

◆

The truth is, as I lay at home alone and unable to socialize or attend Islamic classes and events, I just wanted to die. I thought of the hadith in which the Prophet, *sallallaahu'alayhi wasalam*, said that none of us should wish for death, and I felt ashamed of myself. But I felt utterly incapable of warding off the desire. Sometimes it felt like a desperate need to die because I was convinced that my presence on earth was harmful to my family, my community, the African-American people, and all the Muslims in the world.

What is wrong with you? I'd think to myself during these dark days. *Why can't you be like everyone else?* Then I'd try to convince myself that I should indeed sacrifice my mind, life, and soul in the service of the people and cultures that others said I should. But each time I tried, I felt like I was being choked and suffocated and on the verge of losing my sanity. And deep inside, there was always a voice saying to me, *Hold on. Don't give up. Allah is with you.* But I was so steeped in depression that I would seek refuge in Allah from *Shaytaan*, convinced that this was merely Iblis or one of his helpers trying to fill my heart with pride so that I could end up in the Hellfire.

When I was unable find any rational reason to remain alive, I prayed, *O Allah! If living is best for me, let me live, and if dying is best for me, let me die.* Then I would always wake up the next day, and my heart will fall in sadness and I'd say to myself, *You are only alive because you've committed some sin you haven't atoned for, and Allah knows you would be in Hellfire if He took your soul right now.* Then I would break down crying for how horrible a person I was.

What brings tears to my eyes even today is that, without exception, each time I fell deep into this toxic self-doubt regarding my striving to follow Islamic truth instead religious groups and personalities, Allah gave me some form of reprieve, often from multiple sources. Over and over again, I would have a good dream or someone else would contact me saying they had a good dream about me, or I would receive a call, email, or letter telling me of yet another person who had accepted Islam or returned to practicing the faith after reading one of my books.

Cutting the Commitment Ropes

Today I realize that this "dark period" was one of the immeasurable blessings of Allah. When I had begun to falter on what I knew to be right, He decreed that I became so unwell that I was unable to even be in the presence of people, sects, and communities that were asking me to compromise my soul for group validation. In this way, by making it impossible for me to even be present long enough to be accepted, He was cutting my "commitment ropes" for me.

In this context, I use the term *commitment ropes* to refer to any worldly tie, association, relationship, or lifestyle that we must untangle ourselves from if we are to live in obedience to Allah for the sake of our souls. Throughout life we all have to cut these commitment ropes from time to time, and it is not always easy. In fact, I'm not sure it is ever easy. I have had to make this conscious decision on many occasions, and I continue to. However, some ropes are easier to cut than others.

The epiphany I had as I weathered my spiritual crisis was that it is indeed possible to reduce the collateral damage, emotional wounds, and worldly losses suffered as a result of cutting commitment ropes in life. No, it is not possible to eliminate the damage, wounds, and losses entirely, as spiritual trials are part of the *qadr* of Allah; thus, no one can avoid them. However, I realized that there are so many things we do based on our own conscious (and unnecessary) choices that make the necessary spiritual sacrifices much more difficult and traumatic than they need to be—or that make us completely unwilling to cut the commitment ropes at all.

Here are five ways we can make it easier for ourselves to cut commitment ropes when Allah shows us that we must:

1. **Avoid tying the commitment ropes around your own neck.** In other words, stop making life decisions that are specifically designed to justify your un-Islamic lifestyle, sinful desires, or religious sectarianism to yourself and the world.

    For example, if you struggle with prayer, don't spend your energy writing blogs or social media posts (or creating community groups and projects) aimed at showing how prayer isn't important and how it doesn't make someone Muslim. If Allah tests you with worldly success in this path, especially with multitudes of followers on social media or financial wealth from the project, it's just that much more difficult to let it go when you know you should. In truth, if you tie this commitment rope around your own neck in this way, you are likely to just fall deeper and deeper into self-justification until you become more emboldened on this path and you die in this way.

2. **Make worldly commitments to people and religious commitments to Allah.** This is very important, especially for those who are involved in *da'wah*, those who have studied Islam for many years, those who are considered scholars or sheikhs, or those who make a living off of teaching about Islam. Practically speaking, you achieve this by ensuring that no project you are involved in requires you to say, do, or teach anything that goes against what you genuinely believe is right in front of Allah. In secular contracts, they call this "freedom of speech" or "freedom of religion." But in religious contracts, it is crucial that your finances and living arrangements are not directly tied to you fulfilling very specific demands of a religious group or organization such that they inform you exactly what to say or teach during a speech or class—other than the foundational, clear agreed-upon matters in Islam.

    Whether you work independently or with a religious organization, when you are teaching others, be sure to always clarify and differentiate between religious obligations and religious options and permissible disagreement, as you can put your soul in unnecessary trouble by removing religious concepts from their proper place. Just because an issue or course of action has Islamic evidence for it doesn't mean you are presenting that Islamic evidence in its proper place. Much misguidance is spread as a result of sincere Muslims presenting correct information in incorrect contexts.

By being sure to clarify all of this (religious obligations vs. religious options/disagreement) within yourself and to others, you are making your religious commitment to Allah as you fulfill worldly contracts with people.

3. **Choose your companions and Muslim community carefully and honestly.** Most of us know both the worldly and spiritual adages telling us that we are the company we keep. However, most of us take this information as a means to find people and communities who will reinforce who we already are or want to be, irrespective of whether this companionship or community is good for our lives and souls.

To protect yourself from self-deception, engage in honest self-reflection and prayer to determine whether or not your companions and community reflect what Allah would require or want from you. If you find you have chosen a social circle or community to merely tighten the commitment ropes you tied on your neck, untangle yourself and trust that Allah will grant you something better. For surely, whoever gives up something for the sake of Allah, Allah will replace it with something better.

4. **Find comfort and peace in solitude and independence.** No matter how many friends you have and no matter how much you value your family, job, social network, community, or masjid, it is important that you find comfort and peace in being alone and independent of others. Naturally, this does not mean that we cut ties with family, get rid of our friends, quit our jobs, stop attending Islamic events, or avoid going to the masjid. What this means is that we remain mindful that the spiritual journey we are on is ours and ours alone, and that we are the only soul who will be with us for the entire stretch. Therefore, we need to cultivate a healthy relationship with ourselves such that we engage in self-care and soul-preservation until we become independent of all others except Allah.

Sahl ibn Sa'ad reported that the Angel Gabriel came to the Prophet, *sallallaahu'alayhi wa sallam,* and said, "O Muhammad, live as you wish, for you will die. Work as you wish, for you will be repaid accordingly. Love whomever you wish, for you will be separated. Know that the nobility of the believer is in prayer at night and his honor is in his independence of people" (*al-Mu'jam al-Aswaat* 4410, *hasan* by Al-Albaani).

5. **Nurture your spiritual health daily**, even when you don't feel like it. We nurture our spiritual health by acquainting ourselves with who our Lord is and what He wants from us. The best way to learn this is by reading His book daily and interacting with it. We interact with the Qur'an by reciting it aloud in the way that it was revealed. Also, whenever we come across any *ayaat* discussing Allah's blessings or the people whom He loves, we ask Him to make us amongst them; and whenever we come across any *ayaat* discussing Allah's torment or the people He is displeased with, we ask Allah to protect us from being amongst them. If we feel uninspired to read Qur'an, then read only one *ayah* or a few lines each day.

Most importantly, we nurture our spiritual heath daily by praying our five prayers on time every day with concentration and without exception. We won't get it perfect, but we should still pray, no matter what.

Where Is Your Cave?

When I was forced to withdraw from people and communities and stay home to take care of my physical, emotional, and spiritual health, I felt extremely lonely and alienated. However, I eventually came to think of my solitude like the cave that the believing youth retreated to, as narrated in the Qur'anic *soorah* entitled *Al-Kahf* (The Cave). Like they were compelled to do, I had to remove myself from the world around me for the sake of my soul.

Having a place of spiritual retreat is very important to our ultimate well-being, as even the Prophet had a cave to retreat to in his early days, and the masjid to retreat to for *i'tikaaf* in later years. In life, we all need some time alone to think, clear our heads, and reconnect with our Lord. This is best achieved away from people if possible.

When I was compelled to retreat to my spiritual "cave" and heal, I was able to focus on my Lord, read the Qur'an in solitude, pray, and make *du'aa* such that Allah renewed my strength and dedication to what is right.

During this time, I realized that no matter what mistakes I would inevitably make in life, there is no misguidance on a path that is centered around obeying Allah and His messenger (peace be upon him) while striving my level best to follow whatever I understood to be true and leave alone whatever I understood to be falsehood. As I reminded myself over and over again during this difficult time and wrote in my journal: *Islam is not about always being right. It's about remaining on the right path.*

Nevertheless, this path was very lonely and painful, and in my lowest moments, I sometimes wondered if Allah was really there for me. But when I asked myself this, Allah allowed me to read and reflect on these words from His Book:

"And when My servants ask you concerning Me, indeed I am near.
I respond to the prayer of the supplicant when he calls upon Me.
So let them respond to Me [by obedience]
and believe in Me that they may be [rightly] guided."
—*Al-Baqarah* (2:186)

7

I Didn't Want To Pray

♦

"I find that filling the heart with love of Allah before praying [or doing any good] is one of the most impossible and stressful pieces of advice I've ever heard. Personally, hearing this only makes me feel worse, like I'm a bad Muslim since I don't feel that all the time, and certainly not every time it's time to pray. But knowing that Allah doesn't require me to be perfect when I stand in front of Him in Salaah *is a much more merciful perspective. And,* alhamdulillah, *it also happens to be the true, Islamic perspective. So that's what I prefer to hold on to, the merciful truth, instead of an impossible, stressful standard I could never uphold."*
—Umm Zakiyyah discussing the blog, "I'm Muslim and Don't Pray. What Should I Do?"

Whenever Allah gave me good dreams or comfort in reading Qur'an during my difficult times, it was always with a reminder to remain on the path of *Tawheed*, prayer, Qur'an, *du'aa*, and obedience to Him. In other words, through my good dreams and the dreams of others, and through my reading and reflecting on the Words of Allah, I was consistently reminded that I am a servant of Allah striving upon the right path, not a saint or angel promised infallibility or absolution from my wrongs.

By the mercy of Allah, I understood quite well that "sainthood" did not exist, as all human beings will have to stand before Allah and answer for their time on earth, and no one was guaranteed protection from Hellfire no matter what lofty religious titles or spiritual stations they—or their followers—imagined for them in this world. Unless one was a prophet or one of the righteous people mentioned by name in the Qur'an and Sunnah, we could never claim to be even amongst the *awliyaa'* of Allah—those righteous people with whom Allah is so pleased that He called them His friends and helpers.

But I prayed for it.

As I supplicated to Allah for this immense honor, I knew I would never know until the Day of Judgment if I would be counted amongst these honored servants. I also knew that if I were granted this honor, it wouldn't be because of my inherent goodness, righteous deeds, or anything that I deserved. It would because of Allah's mercy alone.

I knew that I was far from perfect, as I was full of faults and sins, like all other children of Adam. I also knew that what I knew of myself was only a fraction of what Allah knew of me. So I asked Him to forgive me, have mercy on me, and cover my faults.

In the meantime, I was struggling to just *pray*.

Prayer Became a Burden

My lofty hopes for myself were amongst the last traces of *tawakkul* left in my heart during this difficult time. In the Islamic classes I had benefited most from, I had learned that no goal was too big for Allah, no matter how big it appeared to us. So I kept that in mind and made *du'aa* to be amongst the *awliyaa'* of Allah even as I felt barely able to be Muslim.

After scrambling to hold on to my *emaan* itself, the weightiest burden I was carrying was my dreading the *Salaah*. To put it bluntly, I just didn't want to pray, and I had to continuously fight the *waswas* that was trying to convince me that prayer wasn't as important as I thought it was. As I battled these whispers, I dragged myself to prayer, sometimes combining *Dhuhr* and *Asr* and *Maghrib* and *Ishaa* and sitting during each because I was struggling with my physical health at the same time.

During this internal battle, I was tested with coming across a blog that effectively said that those who aren't praying shouldn't burden themselves with prayer and should instead focus on connecting to Allah by reciting *dhikr* to prepare themselves for when their hearts are ready to pray. This was such a huge *fitnah* for me, as it corresponded with the *waswas* I was fighting. Just reading the words took some of the last bit of spiritual energy out of me such that I felt unable to pray, since I now didn't "have to."

It was the result of my own internal battle and spiritual reminders to myself about *Salaah* during this time that ultimately inspired the blog "I'm Muslim and Don't Pray. What Should I Do?"

How I Reclaimed My Faith

"And seek help through patience and prayer, and indeed, it is difficult except for the humbly submissive [to Allah]."
—Qur'an, *Al-Baqarah* (2:45)

Show Up, Let Allah Do the Rest

As I struggled with *Salaah*, often feeling empty inside as I just went through the motions, I reminded myself of this simple truth about obligatory prayer: *Your presence is more important than your perfection.*

In my journal I wrote a reminder to myself to keep going and never give up:

Struggling in your emaan?
Do you feel dead inside when you pray, make du'aa, or read Qur'an?
Remember this: It's okay to show up empty. Just be sure to show up.
And your Lord will fill your heart with the spiritual fuel it needs, eventually.
But you have to show up.
Show up to prayer.
Show up to du'aa.
Show up to Qur'an.
Just the act of showing up is a powerful act of faith.
Allah will take care of the rest.

But What's the Point?

Prayer is the point. Even if you gain nothing from standing in prayer except that the angels have written that you stood in prayer, then that's powerful—and much better than giving up entirely and thus falling into *kufr* and leaving Islam.

Prophet Muhammad (peace be upon him) said, "Between us [the believers] and them [the disbelievers] is the prayer, and whoever leaves it falls into *kufr*" (Al-Tirmidhi, *saheeh*).

The Prophet also said, "What is between a person and committing *shirk* (associating partners with Allah) and *kufr* (disbelief) is abandoning the prayer" (Sahih Muslim).

He also said, "The first matter that the servant [of Allah] will be brought to account for on the Day of Judgment is the prayer. If it is sound, then the rest of his deeds will be sound. And if it is bad, then the rest of his deeds will be bad" (Al-Tabarani; *saheeh*, Sahih al-Jami).

Allah says what has been translated to mean:

> **"Certainly, the believers have succeeded, those who are during their prayer humbly submissive."**
> —*Al-Mu'minoon* (23:1-2)

No, I definitely wasn't amongst those were humbly submissive in prayer, but I was making *du'aa* for it, just like I was praying to be amongst the *'awliyaa*.

8
I Didn't Like 'Muslim Things'

♦

*"After stressing over being such a horrible person, I finally gave up...
I gave up comparing myself to 'good Muslims' and faced the reality of who I was. I gave up trying to find excuses for my laziness, and told myself I needed to be better. And most importantly, I gave up thinking I could lift myself up, and I asked my Lord to lift me up instead."*
—from the journal of Umm Zakiyyah

As I struggled to regain my *emaan*, I realized that I had become a different person, someone I didn't recognize completely. Some of this was good, some of this was problematic, but I think most of it was just the natural progression of moving forward with life and uncovering who I really was deep inside.

On the positive side, as I began to come out of my spiritual confusion, I became more aware of the toxic relationships in my life, and I made a conscious decision to engage in self-care and prioritize my soul above all else, even people I loved. Consequently, I removed myself from toxic relationships, business projects, and environments that were unhealthy for my mental, emotional, and spiritual health.

By far, after connecting to Allah and holding on to my *emaan* independent of religious sects and elitism, making the choice to remove toxic people and environments from my life was the best decision I have ever made. As cliché as it sounds, this decision introduced me to a level of internal peace and happiness that I didn't even know existed in this worldly life. No, I do not mean that all my problems and sadness miraculously disappeared. I mean that as I faced the natural trials, pain, and struggles that were inevitable in life, I experienced for the first time a level of peace, happiness, and joy that only comes from engaging in genuine self-care and soul-preservation—minus the toxicity.

I educated myself on healing emotional wounds, overcoming complex PTSD, and maintaining authentic spirituality without the shackles of manmade rules. Allah also brought into my life a very small circle of friends and loved ones who helped and supported my healing. One has been so instrumental and phenomenal to my emotional and spiritual healing process that I call this person "my Miracle." Because I consider this person, literally, a gift from God. May Allah bless them and grant them the best in this world and in the Hereafter.

As I moved forward in my healing, however, there were setbacks that made fully practicing Islam difficult for me. Because I had spent so long in environments of religious elitism, I was easily triggered whenever I encountered anything or anyone who reminded me of the mind control and spiritual abuse that fuel these groups.

For example, hearing a Muslim lecturer speak with an Arab accent, reading a post about African-Americans needing to "stick together," coming across a book about someone labeled a "saint", seeing a video by a sheikh claiming himself or someone else to be amongst the *awliyaa'* of Allah, happening upon a blog about the arrogance of "commoners" rejecting the "spiritual superiority" of scholars, or encountering anything by a man discussing women's hijab and her "obligation" to make men's lives easier. All of these things consistently triggered anxiety, anger, or physical sickness in me. Sometimes they triggered all three.

In my logical mind, I knew these things had no meaningful connection to my relationship with my Lord and my duty to Him. But in my inner world of unhealed emotional wounds, these experiences reminded me of why I had felt I could no longer be Muslim. *I can't do this anymore!* my internal world screamed. *I can't deal with these people! Oh my God, what if I* do *have to give up my mind, life and soul to these narcissists in order to be a real Muslim?*

As the paranoia took over me, I would seek refuge in Allah from *Shaytaan* to help me fight the thoughts. However, as these triggers became more frequent and unexpected, I educated myself more on practical ways to heal from this aspect of emotional trauma. I continued to seek refuge in Allah and make *du'aa*, but I also began breathing exercises, more journaling, and talking myself through the more difficult episodes. I also frequently spoke to "my Miracle" for advice and coaching, as this helped tremendously.

Through these practical exercises and honest reflections, I realized that I associated "Muslim things" with betrayal, abandonment, slander, verbal abuse, harassment, and lack of emotional safety. To aid in my healing, I anonymously joined some support groups online and found that there were so many others going through what I was experiencing, though none of them were Muslims. One person had a very similar experience to me, except hers was from a community of atheists who punished her for associating with religion or religious people in any way. Another was from a non-religious family deeply involved in pedophilia and sex-trafficking. Another was from a Christian community rooted in religious elitism. Yet we were all suffering the same symptoms.

Finding these survivors of trauma helped me in ways I cannot fully express. What was profound was that we had all been taught the same thing about "those in authority over us": we had no right to our own minds, lives, and souls. And we were all punished in some way if we showed the slightest bit of independence and self-care. Those who were atheist or non-religious were mentally shackled through their abusers' self-serving definitions of unconditional love, and those who believed in God and were part of specific faith traditions were mentally shackled through their abusers' self-serving definitions of spirituality and piety.

One day, as I was reading the Qur'an, I had an epiphany. In Arabic, the word *deen* is often translated as *religion*, but it more accurately describes a life path inspired by what someone believes internally about what is right or wrong in life. And Allah says what has been translated to mean, **"Let there be no compulsion in *deen*."** (*Al-Baqarah*, 2:256).

I realized at that moment that what all of these elitist, abusive systems shared (whether religious, secular or atheist) was going against the divine commandment to not compel anyone to live upon a *deen*—a path or lifestyle—that they did not want or choose for themselves. In other words, these abusers removed from the human being the fundamental God-given right to live according to this maxim: *Whenever you genuinely believe that serving, pleasing, or obeying someone will harm your life and soul, honor your life and soul.*

How I Reclaimed My Faith

"I am trying to expose the fallacy that spiritual practice can do away with the necessity of 'emotional practice.' We cannot be healthy human beings without accepting and experiencing the full range of human feelings."
—Pete Walker, *The Tao of Fully Feeling: Harvesting Forgiveness Out of Blame*

Learning to Feel Again

I don't know why, but during my most difficult trial, Allah chose to test me with both emotional wounding and spiritual crisis at the same time. Till today, I am still in the process of healing. But I am learning to accept my struggle for what it is instead of trying to figure out why I faced it in the first place. As I penned in my journal: *It's not always about a problem to be solved. Sometimes it's about a struggle to be embraced.*

I am still triggered from time to time, and there are still "Muslim things" that are difficult for me because they remind me of what I suffered in communities steeped in spiritual abuse and mind control. To survive these moments, I focus on what Allah has obligated for me, and I don't stress over the *what if*'s and endless "doubtful matters" that so many Muslims argue about.

First and foremost, I prioritize avoiding *kufr* and *shirk* and anything that is clearly *haraam* in my faith. I also focus on the five pillars of Islam and the six pillars of *emaan* and striving my level best to fulfill the conditions of each. Regarding the "Muslim things" that people discuss regarding doubtful matters, I strive to stay away from the arguments as best I can and just live my life. I've lived enough to know that these arguments are never ending, and that most are fueled more by pride and ignorance than by sincerity and knowledge. And Allah knows best.

I certainly have my own list of "doubtful matters" that I stay away from, but other than discussing the necessity to protect our beliefs and worship from doubtful concepts, I don't share my personal limits publicly. I remember how stressful it was for me to hear Islamic teachers speak about their personal opinions on permissible disagreement, thereby stating or implying that others should have the same restrictions; and I don't want to put that mental and spiritual burden on those who trust me.

In my spiritual practice, I focus on the "Muslim things" I know I'm supposed to do, even when it's difficult; and I strive to stay far away from micromanaging anyone else's life and choices. When it comes to the clear teachings of the Qur'an and Sunnah, I will certainly speak up, *bi'idhnillaah*, and unapologetically. But other than that, I don't have much to say, as I believe that other than fulfilling the obligations, every Muslim's life path will be unique, and should be.

However, living upon this spiritual path isn't a simple, smooth process. There are a lot of emotions involved in any life path we choose. And unfortunately, we live in a world where so many people are trying to control and disrupt the paths of others. So focusing on myself and working through the natural agonies of life are daily struggles. But I'm learning to pick my battles and "just breathe" through the pain that is inevitable. Because living as a practicing Muslim is not easy in this world, even amongst Muslims. But I find solace in knowing that there is reward in even this.

In my journal, I wrote:

You're not getting to Paradise without the pain. So stop looking for ways to numb it, suppress it, or escape it; and start looking for ways to bear it with beautiful patience.
Until you meet your Lord.

In this way, I'm learning to *feel* again and to not try to rush myself through the more difficult parts of my life path. It is what it is. So if I want *Jannah*, I'm going to have to take the aches and bruises that come along with getting there.

Stay Active, Not Motivated

Another lesson I'm learning and re-learning over and over again is that I don't have to always want the good, but I do need to *do* the good. And as long as I *want* to want the good, I'm doing okay *insha'Allah*. It's when we don't even *want* to want the good that we have a problem.

So even when I'm struggling with wanting to do "Muslim things," I just focus on staying active, not motivated. Allah is in charge of hearts, so I turn to Him and ask Him to heal my heart.

In my journal, I reflect on asking Allah to help me during my struggles:

When I was at my lowest, I prayed a "contradictory prayer," one that was infused with so much goodness that it contradicted nearly everything I felt and believed about myself at the time...

If I felt dread or laziness at the time for prayer, I prayed, "O Allah, make my joy the Salaah*!" If I could not wrap my heart or mind around something I knew I should do, I prayed, "O Allah, increase me in knowledge and understanding, and make me love what You love."*

Some might call it the prayer of a hypocrite, because my words were so far from my actions.

But even so, Allah hears and answers even the supplication of one who struggles with sincerity and steadfastness upon what is right...so long as they have faith in the One who removes all diseases of the heart.

So have faith, dear soul, and turn to your Lord for help.

You cannot heal your own heart, and you cannot guide yourself upon the right path.

Regarding the need to pace ourselves as we strive upon this noble spiritual path, I wrote:

A friend of mine once said, "Islam is a marathon, not a sprint." These words remind me of the hadith, "...Whoever overburdens himself in his religion will not be able to continue in that way." So we need to find that personal pace that will allow us to have faith in our hearts for the "last lap"—when we cross the finish line of death.

You Have Already Won

Jannah (Paradise) is not for perfect people. It is for the sinful who, in the end, didn't give up on themselves or their Lord. This is something I penned in my journal. And it's true.

Do you believe in Allah? Are you striving upon this path? Are you trying to do good, even as you are imperfect at times? Then receive glad tidings, for Allah says what has been translated to mean:

"And give good tidings to those who believe and do righteous deeds that they will have gardens [in Paradise] beneath which rivers flow..."
—Al-Baqarah (2:25)

9

Why Does Allah Allow That?

♦

"A part of believing that only God can judge is accepting (in word and deed) that only He can speak with authority on what is right or wrong in religious matters. So if your thoughts and lifestyle don't reflect His judgments, then at least be respectful enough to keep silent and hide your sins."
—from the journal of Umm Zakiyyah

Perhaps the only thing worse than feeling like you can't be Muslim anymore is actually pushing yourself over the edge—by allowing your mind, tongue, and life choices to bury you in *kufr*, until when Allah calls you back to *emaan*, you say "No," then nail the coffin shut.

This is how I think of what was possibly the most dangerous part of my spiritual crisis. This was when my mind and heart were overcome with so many questions and doubts that how I responded to them would determine whether or not I would be Muslim at all. It is one thing to not feel like praying or doing "Muslim things," but it is another matter entirely to place yourself as judge and jury of the Lord of the Worlds, and imagine you have that right.

Often this "judge and jury" mindset occurs when we begin to ask "Why does Allah allow such-and-such?" or "Why did the Prophet do such-and-such?" But these questions are not rooted in mere whispers of *Shaytaan* that we can ward off, and they're not rooted in genuine curiosity or hope for clarification to settle our hearts. They're rooted in the assumption that something Allah has mandated or allowed in Qur'an or decreed for His Prophet is incorrect, unfair or wrong—and that the ideas in our own minds and hearts are better for ourselves, our faith and humanity as a whole.

This is the spiritual disaster I was falling into as I allowed my mind and heart to question the teachings of the Qur'an and the life of the Prophet (peace be upon him). What scared me about this experience was that I already knew how this indulgence ended for most people. I had seen so many other Muslims go through it and come out on the other side, and "the other side" offered only three possibilities:

1. Outright disbelief
2. Remaking Islam in your own image
3. Repenting and submitting to authentic Islamic practice

I wanted my ultimate fate to be number 3, but I feared that I would end up with number 1 or number 2.

Outright Disbelief

It's funny the things that come to mind when you are facing fundamental questions of faith that will determine your fate in this world and in the Hereafter. For me, I thought of the NFL player I discussed at the beginning of the book who had left Islam and converted to Christianity. And despite my own spiritual crisis, I knew I didn't want to end up like him.

I also thought of a former friend of mine who had left Islam and joined the church. Specifically, I recalled a picture she had posted of herself on social media. Her head was bowed, her eyes were shut, and her hands were raised as she sang praises to her "Lord and Savior." In front of her was a large painting of a blue-eyed white man with long blond hair who looked like one of my history professors. It was one of the saddest, most heart-wrenching things I'd ever seen. So I knew I didn't want to end up like her.

The truth was, there was no real threat of me joining the church despite my own spiritual doubts. No matter how many questions I had about Islam, I knew I'd only end up with more as a Christian. When I was a teenager, I had spent some time reading the Bible and trying to determine whether I not I wanted be Muslim. My parents had converted to Islam but said that my siblings and I were not Muslims just because they were. Consequently, I went through a brief period in which I studied Judaism and Christianity to examine my heart for what I genuinely believed. I ended up choosing Islam.

In retrospect, I think my focusing on the NFL player and my former friend was a means to distract me from the real threat in front of me. As far as my spiritual fate was concerned, it didn't matter whether I joined the church, became a Buddhist, or professed atheism. Each path would land me in Hellfire—eternally—and that's the reality I wasn't ready to face.

But why did Allah allow such-and such? my mind and heart would demand. The questions were so incessant and heartfelt that merely seeking refuge in Allah from *Shaytaan* didn't satisfy me. I realized that these questions were coming from the depths of my heart and mind, and I needed answers, no matter where this course of action took me.

So while asking Allah to help me, I began reading and researching the issues that weighed most heavily on me. Naturally, there were some questions that were generally philosophical in nature, like questions surrounding *qadr* and the fate of humans on the Day of Judgment and why so many entered Hellfire. Unfortunately, there were no tangible answers regarding these confounding events, at least not ones that could adequately satisfy the human heart and mind. They were beyond human comprehension.

Regarding this, I reminded myself of the *ayah* in the Qur'an: **"He [Allah] cannot be questioned as to what He does, while they [humans and jinn] will be questioned"** (*Al-Anbiyaa'*, 21:23).

Allah also advised: **"O you who believe! Ask not about things which, if made plain to you, may cause you trouble."** (*Al-Maa'idah*, 5:101).

So I accepted that there were some aspects of the human soul and its earthly journey that I would never understand.

Remaking Islam in Your Image

As I combined *du'aa* and research to assist me in working through the difficult questions about Islam that did have tangible answers in this life, I slowly but surely got satisfactory answers. However, there was one consistent temptation pulling at me during this process and represented how so many other Muslims respond to similar spiritual trials: remake Islam in our own image.

In other words, here is where our commitment ropes (that I discussed earlier) become our nooses. Instead of aligning ourselves with the religion of Allah, we align the religion of Allah with ourselves. Then we create projects, organizations, blogs, and "social justice" campaigns around our new faith, which we call *Islam*.

Often these new religious beliefs are just glorified victim doctrines established for the purpose of "glorifying" ourselves in divine texts. This is commonly the pitfall of those of us who have suffered wrongdoing or abuse at the hands of the religious elite or cultures of privilege. As I mentioned in my other writings on the topic, I use the term ***glorified victim*** to refer to anyone who, in response to mistreatment or bigotry, devises and/or propagates new religious teachings or scriptural interpretations that are specifically designed to favor or "glorify" the victim in religious contexts.

These teachings often purport to challenge existing systems of privilege within a faith tradition while in reality they merely create a new faith tradition— or they serve as direct opposition to faith traditions. In other words, a glorified victim is someone who responds to wrongdoing with a greater wrongdoing: opposing God, religion, or spiritual truths themselves. In my blog "Are You a Glorified Victim?" I explain further:

> As a general rule, new belief systems or religious interpretations born from a glorified victim status have at their roots doctrines that arise *in response to circumstance* as opposed to doctrines that *stand on their own* regardless of circumstance. [Thus] many glorified-victim religions manifest themselves as some form of anti-racism or anti-bigotry.
>
> Nevertheless, the religion of the glorified victim should not be confused with faiths that include anti-racism or anti-bigotry as part of their teachings. Glorified-victim doctrine is *based on* anti-bigotry, even

at the expense of religious truth, whereas authentic religious doctrine is based on God's revelations, which by definition *is* religious truth.

Today, some popular glorified-victim doctrines include atheism (which is in fact a religion despite popular opinion otherwise), the Nation of Islam, progressivism/modernism, radical feminism, and LGBTQ religious movements.

Naturally, some of these doctrines are entire religions in themselves whereas others merely claim to be under the umbrella of established faiths. However, what they all have in common is that none of the glorified-victim doctrines view documented divine teachings as the final measure of truth and falsehood or right and wrong, and they all defend their fundamental beliefs by pointing to the wrongdoings, privileges, or inconsistencies/contradictions of other groups or belief systems.

Atheism points to God and religion; the Nation of Islam points to white people; progressivism/modernism points to fundamentalism and traditionalism; radical feminism points to misogyny, sexism, and patriarchy; and LGBTQ movements point to heterosexual privilege.

However, ultimate religious truth points to only God and His messengers.

Repentance and Authentic Islamic Practice

In reflecting on the difficulty in holding on to my *emaan* in an environment in which invitations to disbelief came from all sides, including from those claiming to be part of my own faith, I wrote this journal entry:

The most dangerous enemies to your soul won't come in the form of arrogant media-type personalities, whose cruel words about your faith make you cringe. They will come to you in the form of people you love and trust, who will—like Iblis did with our father Adam—swear to you that they only want what's best for you...and they may believe they actually do.

How I Reclaimed My Faith

"So woe to those who write the Scripture with their own hands, then say, 'This is from Allah,' in order to exchange it for a small price. Woe to them for what their hands have written and woe to them for what they earn."
—Qur'an, *Al-Baqarah* (2:79)

◆

Guard Your Tongue Until the Day of Judgment

Fortunately, my doubts and confusion calmed considerably as I realized the grave danger I was falling into by giving these questions too much attention. Yes, for those questions that had readily available answers in the Qur'an and Sunnah, I sought the answers through research and prayer. However, for those questions that were purely philosophical in nature, I told myself this: *Refrain from speaking about Allah that of which you have no knowledge. If after you die and meet Allah, you still have these questions, then ask Him about them on the Day of Judgment. But for now, get to work so that you can enter Paradise after you die.* For Allah says what has been translated to mean, **"[They will be raised up] in order that He may manifest to them the truth of that wherein they differ"** (*An-Nahl*, 16:39).

You Don't Want To Be at War with Your Lord

In my book *Faith. From the Journal of Umm Zakiyyah*, I write:

> O dear soul, you do not want to be at war with your Lord.
> Did you not read, "Woe to those who write the Book with their own hands then declare, 'This is from Allah!'" (2:79)
> We read these *ayaat* as if they are tales of the ancients, of a people who died long ago with no connection to us. Then we close the Book and declare what is *halaal* or *haraam* based on the flimsy desires of our hearts—or on what is most pleasing to the cultures in which we live.
> But O dear soul, do you wish to be at war with your Lord?
> If we are too lazy to pray, we declare that true Islam exists only in the heart.
> If we wish to cast aside hijab, we declare that the Qur'an requires only that we "dress modestly."
> If we do not want our husbands to marry another wife—or our wives to think we ever would—we declare that polygamy is not allowed in our times.
> If we wish to deny the permissible disagreement surrounding music—or any other *ikhtilaaf* issue we refuse to see as such—we declare that anyone who believes it is *haraam* is an extremist, or that love of Allah and His Book cannot exist in the heart of those believe it is not.
> And on and on, we recite the words of men as if they are the Words of Allah.
> Meanwhile the angels are recording in our Book of Deeds every word that we utter.

Then we open the Book of Allah and read about those who speak about Allah that of which they have no right or knowledge, and we actually wonder who they are.

10
What If I Die As a Disbeliever?

◆

"Faith is accepting that, ultimately, the good doesn't come from you. So when you feel yourself slipping, turn to the One who guided you in the first place. He will help you. He always does, if it truly His help you seek."
—from the journal of Umm Zakiyyah

The scary thing about gaining back some semblance of faith after spiritual crisis is the knowledge of how close you came to letting it all go. That "close call" isn't something that is easily forgotten, and perhaps it shouldn't be. Because you now know on a deeply personal level the fragility of the human heart and the inevitable ups and downs of *emaan*. You also know, all too well, how you can be living your life thinking everything is just fine, only to, in a split second, fall into the treacherous waters of disbelief. And as you flail your arms and desperately gasp for air, you find that there is no one reaching out a hand to save you.

This is a frightening reality, and I don't imagine that the memory of my own spiritual trepidation is leaving my mind or heart any time soon.

But what this terrifying experience left me with was this question: *What if you die as a disbeliever anyway?* And honestly, I don't have an answer.

How I Reclaimed My Faith

"Sometimes your heart has to cry out in agony before it falls in humble submission."
—from the journal of Umm Zakiyyah

◆

I know, as a Muslim, that I'm not supposed to entertain *what if* questions, as they are generally from *Shaytaan*. But entertaining the possibility of dying as a disbeliever was difficult for me to fight. Because my logical mind said: *You can say it is a whisper from* **Shaytaan** *if you like, but that doesn't mean you have any* guarantee that you will not die as a disbeliever and end up in Hellfire forever. And then, what was all of this for?

I didn't really have an answer to this because I was still warding off the fear that I couldn't even be Muslim. Because if there is anything my spiritual crisis taught me, it is how terrifyingly weak I really am.

Allah Is Carrying You

In reflecting on the possibility of dying upon disbelief, this is the epiphany that came to my heart: *Allah is carrying you; you are not carrying you.* And He is All-Powerful, All Capable. So I focused on trusting that He would take my soul as a believer.

To appeal to my logical mind, I reminded myself of the times that I had wanted to die and prayed to Allah, *O Allah! If living is best for me, let me live, and if dying is best for me, let me die.* And each time, I woke up and lived another day. So if I were really under the threat of dying as a disbeliever, Allah would have taken my soul then, in response to my prayer. For surely dying as a Muslim in the throes of depression is much better than dying as a disbeliever in any state. So because I'm alive today, I know my Lord has plans for me, and none of them include taking my soul in any state other than *emaan*.

Allah says:

> **"By the glorious morning light, and by the night when it is still,**
> **Your Guardian Lord has not forsaken you,**
> **nor is He displeased..."**
> —*Adh-Dhuhaa* (93:1-3)

Glory is to You, O Allah, and praise is to You. I bear witness that nothing has the right to be worshipped except You alone. I seek Your forgiveness and repent to You.

Anything that I have said in this book that is truthful or beneficial is from my Lord alone, and all praises and thanks belong to Him. And anything that I have said that is mistaken or harmful in any way, then this is from myself or Shaytaan, and I ask Allah to forgive me for it. And I ask the reader to also forgive me, and to ask my Lord to forgive me. I also ask that Allah accepts me and all who read this to be amongst those whom He loves, though we could never do anything to deserve this immense honor. And O Allah, I beg you by your Mercy and Generosity, to take us as believers, and grant us Jannah without account!

Be Careful What You Feed Your Soul

◆

In closing, I want to implore all readers who wish to meet Allah with *emaan* in their hearts to value your souls above all else. In this world, if you choose to walk the path of the practicing Muslim, you will be harassed, abused, and called many offensive names, sometimes by professed Muslims themselves. Extremist, Wahhabi, homophobe, transphobe, bigot, intolerant. These are just a few names that those who oppose our faith use to refer to those who strive upon authentic Islam in hopes of meeting their Lord with *emaan* in their hearts.

While there are certainly real extremists and bigots who call themselves Muslim and set out to harm and mistreat those who live a different life path, you should not waste your energy trying to convince the world that you are not amongst them. Yes, whenever you get the opportunity, clarify the real teachings of your faith, most specifically the prohibitions against harming the innocent and using force or violence to compel someone to become Muslim, but do not make this back-and-forth your focus. And most importantly, do not allow the culture of anti-Muslim bigotry to dictate the narrative of your faith that you share with the world. The truth of Islam stands on its own, and trust that anyone who sincerely wants guidance will accept it, with or without your help.

At a certain point, we have to accept that there will always be those more interested in name-calling and bullying than in genuine understanding and truth. Unfortunately, as we are in the Last Days, this group is more common than those whose hearts are sincerely interested in learning who you are and what you believe. Allah says,

> "...And you will surely hear from those who were given the Scripture before you and from those who associate partners with Allah much abuse. But if you are patient and fear Allah, indeed, that is of the matters (worthy) of determination."
> —*Ali'Imraan* (3:186)

Yes, we should share Islam with others, but let's not forget that *da'wah* in both meaning and practice is only an invitation. Just like any invitation you give someone, it is not your job to obsess over whether or not they accept it—or even whether or not they see as good what you're inviting them to. Once you've given them the invite in the kindest, clearest language possible and delivered it in the way that they are most likely to open it and sincerely consider it, leave them alone and go one with your life.

As for the hostile anti-Muslim environment that we are tested with living in and the claims of "compassion and tolerance" that so many Muslims run after in seeking approval of those who mock our faith, I share this quote from my book *Faith. From the Journal of Umm Zakiyyah*:

> We like to refer to the prophetic example in times like this, especially when advocating for compromises in our faith under the guise of "compassion and tolerance." But let's not forget, our prophet of mercy was slandered, boycotted, fought, and called horrible names too, even as he did everything possible to show compassion and tolerance as he spoke the truth.
>
> But it wasn't his compassion and tolerance that they had a problem with. It was his truth. God's truth.
>
> During his era, the disbelievers would've been more than happy for him to leave off compassion and tolerance, if it meant giving up Islam and following their belief systems.
>
> After all, they certainly left off compassion and tolerance when dealing with *him*.
>
> So no, it never was about compassion and tolerance. It was about playing politics and word games to make good appear evil, and truth appear false.
>
> Nothing has changed.
>
> They didn't want his compassion and tolerance—and they don't want ours. They want our hearts and souls. (And sadly, some of us are giving it to them.)
>
> Yes, we will continue to show compassion and tolerance. Because it is what God instructs of us.
>
> And it's the right thing to do.
>
> But at a certain point, you're going to have to accept that it really doesn't matter whether or not others are pleased with you. Let it suffice that your Lord is pleased with you.
>
> So leave them to their name-calling, slandering, and political word games. It's all they have. This is their Paradise, after all.
>
> Yours is in the Hereafter—if you want it.
>
> Don't sacrifice it for the fleeting comfort and disingenuous acceptance they offer to you on earth.

Some Closing Remarks

And finally, I share these last words of advice from a blog that I posted some time ago: Most of us understand the psychological and emotional harm that comes from constantly exposing ourselves to negative, toxic social and personal environments. So we limit interactions with negative people, and we end toxic relationships. But when it comes to religion, we say things like, "If you truly have faith, nothing can shake it."

There was a time when I myself believed this and proclaimed the same. But today when I hear statements that attest to the unshakeable nature of "true faith," what comes to mind is the popular saying, "Fools rush where wise men wouldn't dare to tread."

Even the Prophet (peace be upon him) prayed, "O You who turns hearts, make my heart firm upon Your religion" (Tirmidhi, *saheeh* by Al-Albaani). In the Qur'an, Allah describes the believers as those who pray, **"Our Lord, let not our hearts deviate after You have guided us; and grant us from Yourself mercy. Indeed You are the Bestower"** (*Ali 'Imraa*n, 3:8).

Also, the Prophet repeatedly warned us about the dangers of bad companionship, and in the Qur'an Allah narrates the story of a person in Paradise reflecting on his time in this world and recalls a friend who would cast doubt on the truth of the Resurrection:

> **"...I had a companion [on earth], who would say, 'Are you indeed of those who believe, that when we have died and become dust and bones, we will indeed be recompensed?' He will say, 'Would you [care to] look?' And he will look and see him in the midst of the Hellfire. He will say, 'By Allah, you almost ruined me! If [it were] not for the favor of my Lord, I would have been of those brought in [to Hell].'"**
> —*As-Saffaat* (37:51-57)

And bad companionship does not come only in the form of friendships. It also comes in the form of our social, academic, and work environments. It can also come in the form of what we expose ourselves to through the media, whether for entertainment or listening to "the news."

Naturally, because we live in this earthly world, we interact with friends and neighbors, we go to school and work, and we remain abreast of what is happening around us. However, if we hope for both good in this world and good in the Hereafter, we cannot afford to be only active participants in our worldly pursuits. We must also be active participants in our spiritual pursuits.

In the Qur'an, Allah says:

> **"And among the people is he who says, 'Our Lord, give us in this world,' and he will have, in the Hereafter, no share. But among them is he who says, 'Our Lord, give us the best in this world and the best in the Hereafter, and protect us from the punishment of the Fire.'"**
> —*Al-Baqarah* (2:200-201)

And we gain the best in both worlds, as well as protection from the Fire, by nourishing our hearts and souls with constant remembrance of Allah, prioritizing the five daily prayers, and working everyday to protect ourselves from spiritual degeneration—and by being ever aware of the human weakness in ourselves.

Perhaps it's okay to believe things like, *If you truly have faith, nothing can shake it*—so long as you recognize that true faith does not come from you. It is a gift from Allah. We just need to make sure that our hearts are ready to receive this gift…

By protecting ourselves from toxic relationships and environments that prevent our hearts from being open to Allah's guidance.

So be careful what you feel your soul.

About the Author

Umm Zakiyyah is the bestselling author of the novels *If I Should Speak* trilogy, *Muslim Girl*, and *His Other Wife*; and the self-help book for religious survivors of abuse *Reverencing the Wombs That Broke You*. She writes about the interfaith struggles of Muslims and Christians and the intercultural, spiritual, and moral struggles of Muslims in America. Her work has earned praise from writers, professors, and filmmakers and has been translated into multiple languages.

Umm Zakiyyah holds a BA in elementary education and an MA in English language learning. She studied Arabic, Qur'an, Islamic sciences, *'aqeedah*, and *tafseer* in America, Egypt, and Saudi Arabia for more than fifteen years. She currently teaches *tajweed* (rules of reciting Qur'an) and *tafseer* in Baltimore, Maryland.

Also By Umm Zakiyyah

If I Should Speak
A Voice
Footsteps
Realities of Submission
Hearts We Lost
The Friendship Promise
Muslim Girl
His Other Wife
UZ Short Story Collection
The Test Paper (a children's book)
Pain. From the Journal of Umm Zakiyyah
Broken yet Faithful. From the Journal of Umm Zakiyyah
Faith. From the Journal of Umm Zakiyyah
Let's Talk About Sex and Muslim Love
Reverencing the Wombs That Broke You: A Daughter of Rape and Abuse Inspires Healing and Healthy Family
And Then I Gave Up: Essays About Faith and Spiritual Crisis in Islam

Order information available at ummzakiyyah.com/store

Read more from Umm Zakiyyah at uzauthor.com

www.ingramcontent.com/pod-product-compliance
Lightning Source LLC
Chambersburg PA
CBHW051348040426

42453CB00007B/476